A Bride's Guide

What NOT To Do On Your Wedding Day!

I0039067

How to Avoid Wedding Day Nightmares & Disasters

. . . . .

Tom Grandmaison

Disclaimer

Nobody can guarantee a perfect day, never mind
a perfect wedding day. This book is provided
for educational and entertainment purposes only.
By purchasing a printed copy or downloading an
e-book, it is agreed the author and publisher
are totally free of any subsequent liability by the
implied content of this book.

If you do not agree with this warning, then return
the book or download immediately for a full refund.

Tom Grandmaison
P.O. Box 213
Swansea, MA 02777
www.abridesguidebook.com

Ordering information: Use the above address.

Book layout: Elisabeth Lariviere
Cover photo courtesy of Wave Break Media/Shutterstock

A Bride's guide: how to avoid wedding day nightmares & disasters
/ Tom Grandmaison – 1st edition.

Sunglow Publishing Company

ISBN-13: 978-0-9863102-01
ISBN-10: 09863102-0-4
eBook ISBN-13: 978-0-9863102-1-8
eBook ISBN-10: 0-9863102-1-2

Table of Contents

Introduction

The weather is perfect; the flowers are in full bloom;
everyone is on time; everything is as it should be . . .

Like the realization of a childhood dream, a bride plans her wedding day hoping that everything she dreamed about will come true and her wedding day will be perfect. In reality, a totally glitch-free wedding is nearly impossible. Problems, conflicts, mishaps, oversights and outright disasters with people, places and things can occur. I know. I've seen them.

As a professional photographer, I've attended over fifteen hundred weddings, hoping to capture the great moments that make a wedding special. But I've also been a witness to incidents that everyone would rather forget.

Most wedding related books approach weddings as a "what to do" planner. My book approaches your wedding day as a "what not to do" guide.

I've included over two hundred tales of wedding woes, things that went wrong at real weddings, with suggestions on how they could have been avoided. These are stories you can learn from.

It is my hope that by browsing through this collection of wedding day disasters, you'll gain valuable insight and may achieve that perfect wedding.

—*Tom Grandmaison*

About the Author

Tom Grandmaison is a retired professional photographer. He began photographing weddings while attending college as a fine arts major in the 1970's. Upon graduation, he opened a portrait and wedding photography studio.

During his 35 years as a professional photographer, Tom Grandmaison photographed over 1500 weddings. Most of these candid documentaries covered the entire wedding day as they unfolded. This was quite an education. After witnessing problems at almost every wedding, he started taking notes. He observed what went smoothly and what didn't. He analyzed the mishaps and wrote down solutions. After noticing that many of these same mishaps kept occurring over and over again, he was prompted to write this book:

A Bride's Guide: How to Avoid Wedding Day Nightmares & Disasters.

Acknowledgments

I sincerely would like to thank Kathy Conlon Thoren, Jennifer Glendye Howard, Marc Mancini and Paul Rousseau for their immeasurable help in writing and editing this book.

This book is dedicated to all the wonderful people I have met while photographing weddings for over thirty-five years. Many families opened their homes and their hearts to me, quite often treating me like one of the family while displaying the utmost hospitality. To these people, I send a heartfelt "Thank You".

How to Use This Book

This book is arranged for the most part in the chronological sequence of a typical wedding day.

It begins with the bride and groom getting ready at their respective locations and then some form of transportation, typically limousines, will pick them up and take them to the ceremony location. After this, a formal photography session will usually follow. Next, everyone goes to the reception. When the festivities are over, the newlyweds leave for their honeymoon.

I realize this is not an exact footprint for everyone's wedding. Nonetheless, the majority of the incidents described should still be beneficial regardless of your sequence of events. *Chapter 8 - Throughout the Day* refers to glitches or problems that can surface or be bothersome at any time during the day. It also describes other issues that wouldn't fit into a single category but still needed to be addressed.

I've taken the liberty of using an example that actually took place prior to a wedding day – *The Jack and Jill Shower*. The incident or problem is first described followed by "*My Advice*". The "*My Advice*" section is an analysis on how the mishap may have been avoided and frequently includes alternatives.

THE JACK AND JILL
SHOWER

Plans were made for the engaged couple to attend a wedding shower in their honor. A date was chosen, a hall reserved and the food menu was decided. The bride and groom to be, lived out of town and were scheduled to fly into a local airport. Arriving in the morning, they would attend the shower later in the day. Unfortunately, it was winter and they lived in Chicago, a place known for severe weather. An untimely snow storm canceled their scheduled flight and closed all the airports in the region. They didn't arrive home until the next day. So the Jack and Jill shower went off as planned, but without the guests of honor.

. . . . .

My Advice: This event reeks of bad planning. The logical solution would have been to plan on arriving a day or two earlier. However, with work and school schedules, this is not always possible. When a time cushion is not available, the obvious alternative would be to schedule the event when the weather conditions are more favorable.

CHAPTER 1

EARLY ON THE BIG DAY

BOUTONNIERES
ARE BREAKING

The flowers were delivered and passed out to the groom and groomsmen. When they started pinning them to their lapels, the flower stems started breaking just below the flower. This was a real cause for concern because almost all the boutonnieres broke, not just one or two.

· · · · ·

My Advice: I discussed this situation with a professional florist and was told that this can be caused by using old flowers that were refrigerated too long. However, sometimes when the stem is bent too much as the boutonniere is being pinned, the stem can also break. This is why it's a good idea to have a few extra boutonnieres on hand. It's also helpful to have the florist pin the boutonnieres on when they are delivered. That way the florist can always make a phone call to the flower shop and personally deal with any emergency.

I RIPPED MY PANTS

All the groomsmen were at the groom's house, getting dressed in their formal attire. One member of the wedding party, a rather large man, sat in a chair after he was dressed and burst the seam in the seat of his pants. An emergency call was made to the tuxedo shop while the groomsman waited in his undershorts for his replacement pants to arrive.

· · · · ·

My Advice: Had the groomsman gained weight since his tuxedo fitting? Who knows, but trying on the outfits a few days before the wedding might be the prudent thing to do. Unexpected things happen. Make sure you have the emergency number of the tuxedo shop, as their regular hours might not correspond with your schedule. Also be sure to ask any "what if" questions well before the wedding day.

It's Showtime

The sky opened up and the rain poured down about half an hour before the bride was to leave for the church. Fortunately, it stopped about five minutes before her departure time and the sun came out. The ground, however, was saturated with water and puddles were everywhere. The bride's father was a very tall man who decided to hold his daughter's train as she walked out to the limo. All the neighbors had gathered in front of their homes to watch the bride leave. The bride's dad, in his desire to do a good job, inadvertently held her train and petticoat a little too high. As they walked out, he actually exposed his daughter's backside as she climbed into the limo.

. . . . .

My Advice: It was a nice gesture that dad was being protective of his daughter's gown. After all, he probably paid for it. However, the too tall dad should have left this job to the maid of honor, who was more suited to this task. Everyone with a camera had to use discretion while taking photographs.

POWER DOWN, POWER UP

The bride's family owned a beautiful waterfront estate with a fantastic view in a very prestigious neighborhood. The plan was to have the wedding reception in two very large tents on the family property. After conferring with the rental company, the bride's dad realized that he would need a large source of electrical power in the vicinity of the tents. He hired an electrical contractor to run a powerful 220 volt circuit out to the proximity of the tents. Once this was done, the bride's dad called the rental company. He asked them to come out to the house to make sure that the new electrical service would suffice. They reassured him there would be no problem but they would still send somebody out to the house to check it out. For some reason this was never done. The tent company came out to the house the day before the wedding, set up the tents, but still didn't check out the new electrical service.

Early on the wedding day, someone finally decided to power up and guess what? The brand new electrical outlet didn't fit the plug on the main power line that would feed both the tents. How could this have been overlooked? The bride's dad was furious. The reception was a few hours away and the bride's family had to leave shortly to go to the church ceremony. After a few tense moments and some frantic phone calls, the bride's dad located a large generator mounted on a large flat-bed truck. This vehicle could park in an inconspicuous area and run whatever type of lines out to the tents that were needed. This obviously saved the day.

. . . . .

My Advice: Sometimes your best efforts are sabotaged by someone else's oversight. Make the site inspection a contingency to any equipment or tent rental agreement. The last thing that bride's dad wanted to deal with was an unexpected problem like this. This certainly created unnecessary stress for the bride's family.

THE FLOWERS ARE MISSING

All the flowers were delivered to the bride's home. The plan was for someone to bring the flowers with them to the church. However, in all the confusion, this simple task was neglected. The flowers were forgotten at the bride's house. Upon arriving at the church, this mistake was realized and someone was sent back to the house to retrieve them. In the meantime, the ceremony began and the groom, groomsmen and the groom's parents all participated without their flowers.

. . . . .

My Advice: The ideal scenario would be to have the flowers delivered directly to the church. It would be one less thing to worry about. However, this is not always possible or practical. There's always a lot of excitement, anxiety and confusion at the bride's house. In fact, the larger the wedding party, the greater the confusion. It's absolutely amazing how often something important can inadvertently be left at the bride's house such as flowers, marriage license, makeup, medication, checks, directions, going away outfits, etc. That's why someone should make a final checklist during a quiet moment well before the wedding day.

CHAPTER 2

GETTING READY

A BAD CHOICE

The florist delivered all the flowers to the bride's home at the expected time. The bride handed the bouquets to all the young women. The ring bearer was there as well because his mom was one of the bridesmaids. When it came time to pin on his boutonniere, his mom realized that it was an adult size boutonniere with a three inch straight pin. She started pinning it on his tuxedo lapel which partially obstructed his face and discovered this boutonniere would never work. The ring bearer was a typical fidgety four year old boy and this large pin right over his heart was certainly a recipe for disaster.

. . . . .

My Advice: What was the florist thinking? Was this an oversight on someone's part? Didn't anyone discuss the ring bearer's age? What's wrong with requesting a smaller boutonniere secured with a safety pin? This would be the perfect solution for any very young ring bearers. Avoid a tragedy and discuss this with your florist.

A NEAR MISS

The bride's aunt had a beautiful home right near the church where the wedding was taking place. The groom was from out of town so she offered him the use of her home. This would allow him to get ready in close proximity to the church. The family pet was a small lap dog that found all these strange people in his house very exciting. He ran around the house endlessly, jumping on and off the chairs and sofas.

The groom, while waiting for the rest of the groomsmen to arrive, decided to relax on the sofa. As he sat down someone noticed a puddle of dog urine precariously close to his tuxedo pants. What would he have done if he had sat in it with just a half hour before the ceremony was to begin? To spend your wedding day with dog urine on your pants would have been less than desirable.

. . . . .

My Advice: Pets and weddings usually don't mix. Unless the dog is an integral part of the wedding, securing the pet elsewhere would be the prudent thing to do.

The Wrong Bouquet

When I arrived at the bride's home to take some candid photos, I found the bride crying hysterically in the living room. It seems that the flowers were just delivered to the bride's home a few minutes earlier, and the bride's bouquet was all wrong. This made the photo session next to impossible. When a bride is upset like this no amount of coaching is going to magically change her demeanor.

. . . . .

My Advice: In the bride's mind, her entire wedding day was ruined. It could very well be if she had let it. However, a few important checks would have avoided this disaster. The bride should have received an accurate description of her flowers in writing when she hired the florist. A photo or clipping of the actual arrangement would be even better. Then about a week to ten days before her wedding she should have met with the florist to reconfirm her order in detail. Pay close attention to colors and styles. Every time I have seen this happen, the bride is devastated. Do yourself a favor and stay on top of the details. Tears of joy are one thing but tears of disappointment are never welcome.

THE WATERFALL

It was a cold December evening wedding that took place around the holidays. The bridesmaids and flower girl all wore velour dresses with a holiday flair. The flower girl was about three years old. She also wore white tights with black patent leather shoes and was absolutely adorable. The bride passed out the flowers to the bridesmaids and then gave the flower girl her little basket of flowers. She raised the basket to smell the flowers when a substantial amount of water poured out of the basket. It ran down the front of her dress, saturated her white tights, and filled her shoes with water. She immediately burst into tears. She was cold and miserable. Water and velour are never a good mix. How could this have happened?

. . . . .

My Advice: The basket had a plastic liner. Inside the liner was some floral foam which held water to keep the flowers fresh. The basket was overfilled but the florist had neglected to provide any warning. A large note should have been attached to the basket. This would have alerted the bride of the hazard and a small disaster could have been avoided.

FLOWERS VS. SPAGHETTI STRAPS

The flowers arrived at the bride's home, well before the ceremony. The flowers were beautiful, exactly what she had ordered. She immediately started handing out bouquets to all the bridesmaids. She then attempted to pin a corsage on her mom, but there was one small problem. Mom was wearing a gown with spaghetti straps. Though she was successful in actually pinning the corsage to the thin strap, the corsage would not remain stable and kept flipping around. The thin strap had as much stability as a rubber band. An emergency call was made to the florist to try to remedy the problem. A wrist corsage was delivered to the church.

. . . . .

My Advice: When ordering flowers, consider what attire people will be wearing. Perhaps the bride's mom hadn't selected her dress before the flowers were ordered. Spaghetti straps will never support a pin on corsage. The bride's mom really needed a wrist corsage but that fact wasn't considered until it was almost too late.

FLOWERS VS. THE BROCADE JACKET

The bride's grandmother was wearing an elaborate, very expensive gown with a matching jacket. The jacket had a heavy brocade with rhinestones and a thick, heavy backing. The bride attempted to pin her grandmother's corsage on but the pins bent. She was also worried about damaging her grandmother's outfit if she tried too hard.

. . . . .

My Advice: Once again, a wrist corsage was in order. When ordering flowers, you must consider what people are wearing. The bride's grandmother may as well have been wearing a bullet proof vest.

LACKADAISICAL BRIDE

The bride and the bridesmaids were getting ready at the bride's house. Someone told them it was okay to be fashionable late. The bride and her bridesmaids took as much time as they wanted which resulted in the bride arriving one half hour late for the wedding ceremony.

. . . . .

My Advice: The bride was obviously misinformed on this issue. All the guests had to sit around an extra half hour, waiting for the ceremony to begin. A church ceremony usually can't be condensed. Once you run late, problems multiply. When you are in a hurry, accidents and errors of omission are more likely to occur. You can rarely make up for lost time. Remember, the restaurant or function hall expects the wedding party to be prompt. They have to serve the food at a certain time. Avoid the "it's okay to be late" mentality. It's perfectly fine to get ready in a relaxed frame of mind. Just start early and allow plenty of time for preparation.

SABOTAGE AT THE SALON

The bride and the bridesmaids arrived at the hair salon promptly at 6 AM, the predetermined appointment time. However, the store was closed and there were no lights on. The bride panicked and rightly so. After searching through a local phone book, she located the hair stylist's home phone number and placed a frantic call. After countless rings, a groggy voice answered "Hello?" "Where are you? Why aren't you here?" the bride shrieked. The stylist responded "I'll be right there. My alarm didn't go off."

It was 7:15 AM by the time the hairdresser showed up with dripping wet hair. As the day unfolded, the hairdresser revealed that he had gone out clubbing the evening before and couldn't get up on time. He had placed his social life ahead of his responsibility to his client. Precious time was lost on a very tight schedule. Once the bride starts to run late it is very difficult to catch up.

. . . . .

My Advice: This could have been avoided by taking a few precautionary measures. Ask for the stylist's home or cell number ahead of time. Ask if there's a backup plan if something unexpected happens. Finally, try to find a hairdresser with an assistant or one who networks with other stylists in emergencies.

Most brides have a test run done on their hair prior to the wedding day. If the practice run meets your expectations, have snapshots taken from several angles using daylight to show as much detail as possible. In the event you end up with a backup hairstylist, those photos will be an immeasurable help and you will end up with the look you originally envisioned.

SABOTAGE AT THE BRIDE'S HOUSE

The bride had planned to have the cosmetologist come to her home at 9 AM. Not having to travel to a hair salon would be a big convenience. Nine o'clock came and went, and she didn't show up. By 10 AM she still hadn't appeared or even called the bride. The bride made several attempts to contact her by cell phone but she wasn't answering. One of the bridesmaids had an aunt that was a hair dresser, so an emergency call was made to her. She agreed to save the day and all the girls immediately left the house. This turned out to be a wonderful thing because the sister of the no show cosmetologist called the bride's cell phone at 11 AM. She told the bride that her sister was in an auto accident and couldn't make it to the house.

. . . . .

My Advice: Unless someone was totally unconscious or critically injured, he or she could pick up their cell phone or ask someone else to make the important call to the bride. Once again, a contingency plan should be in effect. The same suggestions as *Sabotage at the Salon* would apply.

THE APPRENTICES

The groom's sister owned a well-established hair and beauty salon. She also taught cosmetology classes at a local school. The plan was that she would style the hair for the bride and bridesmaids, and two of her most experienced stylists would do the makeup. The groom's sister did a masterful job on the women's hair. She was very professional and efficient. However, it was a totally different story with her two assistants. They were very slow and unsure of themselves while applying makeup on the bridal party. This delayed them immeasurably and led to the bride and bridesmaids arriving late for the wedding ceremony.

. . . . .

My Advice: A wedding day isn't the time to be practicing cosmetology skills. The apprentices performed very nonchalantly and took their time like they were in a classroom situation. There's a definite need for efficient wedding day time management. As previously mentioned, it's very difficult to make up lost time. Other wedding related services are also on a tight schedule and have limited flexibility, such as the ceremony location and reception hall.

THE BRIDESMAIDS MAKE A POINT

The bride's bouquet was primarily made of red roses, so each of the girls would be carrying a single red rose. The roses were handed out at the bride's home and all the women removed the little green stem cap that contains a little water to keep it fresh. The excess water was wiped off the stem and then all the young women huddled closer and closer together for a group photo. After a few quick snapshots they dispersed. Much to everyone's horror, the bride had at least two holes in her veil. This was caused by the sharp, angled end of the flower stem, which punctured her veil when the brides-maids crowded around the bride.

. . . . .

My Advice: Flower stems can be quite sharp because they're cut at an angle to better absorb water. Flower management is obviously a cause for concern, so take a good look at what you have and exercise caution.

TOO SHORT FOR THE RAILING

The bride's mom wanted photos of the bride and her two younger sisters, aged six and eight, on the elaborate staircase inside her home. She went ahead and decorated the railing with flowers and ribbons. When the three sisters stood on the staircase, the younger two were not tall enough to look over the railing so they had to look through the spindles. This made it look like they were in jail with the posts covering their faces. Even then, with all the decorations you could hardly see them.

. . . . .

My Advice: When decorating the rail, the bride's mom didn't consider the application in detail. She neglected to consider the children's height. The solution was to have the children stand in front of the railing at the bottom of the stairs with the bride on the stairs directly behind them.

THE BUG EYED BRIDE

The bride decided to use iridescent eye shadow to enhance her makeup. She selected a silvery blue shade. Instead of making her eyes look better, whenever she was exposed to a bright light source such as the sun, a spotlight or a camera flash, the reflection from the eye shadow would make her eyes pop out, giving her a bug eyed look.

. . . . .

My Advice: Eye makeup should enhance the bride's face, not compete with it. Eyelids look best with a darker, smoky earth shade. Darker colors recede and light or bright, shiny colors reflect and/or advance. I realize this is a matter of personal taste, but one only has to see the photographic results of someone wearing really shiny eye shadow and lipstick to witness the surreal quality it creates.

THE FAMILY PET

The bride looked great. Her hair and makeup were impeccable, she was completely dressed and ready to go to the ceremony. She looked like she belonged on a cover of a magazine. The family dog, a medium sized cocker spaniel, was excited by all the commotion and strange people in the bride's home. When the bride entered the living room, the family pet ran across her train and jumped on her gown. The sharp toenails punctured the gown in a few places.

There were a few paw prints as well. The bride was horrified and, as to be expected, burst into tears.

· · · · ·

My Advice: This type of scenario is all too common. As previously mentioned, have the family pet secured in an area away from where the activities will be.

THE FAMILY CANINES

The bride's family owned two large, long haired dogs. I was told that they were both very friendly and very old. Upon arriving at the bride's house, both dogs were sitting between the edge of the living room floor and dining room. This created a big obstacle for the bridesmaids, florist, photographer, videographer, limo driver, relatives and all the people that typically come to the bride's house before the wedding ceremony. The dogs were repeatedly getting in everyone's way and leaving fur all over everyone's formal attire. When someone asked if they could be moved, the bride replied," Oh, that one has arthritis and practically has to be carried. The other one is very old and can hardly walk!" Needless to say, this greatly slowed the whole preparation process down, wasting valuable time. The dogs didn't care whether the bride was getting married or not. It was just another day to them, hanging around the house.

· · · · ·

My Advice: Even though the bride loved the two seventy pound obstacles like family members, she was totally oblivious to the fact that many people were trying to get ready for an important formal event. Having to clean dog hair from an outfit before leaving didn't help either. She could have said goodbye to them before dressing up and had them placed elsewhere. She also could have hired a dog sitter, a family friend or left them at a local kennel. As previously mentioned, it's wise to keep the family pets in a more secluded place.

THE FINAL FINISH

The bride and bridesmaids arrived at the hair salon in several different cars at appointment time. The bride insisted she be styled and arranged last as she didn't want anyone to see her ahead of time. The five bridesmaids were finished and it was the bride's turn to be styled. The bridesmaids drove back to the bride's house where they would get into their dresses and wait for the bride to arrive. As it turned out, the bride's hairstyle and veil were the most challenging and time consuming for the hairstylist. The bride arrived back at her home with her hair and veil looking great. Unfortunately, she still had her jeans on and the ceremony was scheduled to start in ten minutes. She was quick to put her gown on but she still had a twenty-five minute limo ride to church.

. . . . .

My Advice: Requesting that she be styled last was illogical on the bride's part. She should have been the first one to have her hair and makeup done. Her outfit was the most complex and required more preparation time. If one of the bridesmaids had been late, the ceremony could have gone on without her, but not without the bride.

THE FLOWERS MAKE AN IMPRESSION

It was a late spring wedding and the bride had ordered an impressive array of bouquets. They were primarily made of lilies, with the bride's bouquet being the largest and most impressive. After handing out the bouquets to all the bridesmaids, she grabbed her bouquet and then they gathered together for some group photos. When the impromptu photo session was over, they noticed they all had bright golden orange pollen all over their dresses. Of course, it was most noticeable on the bride's gown. The moisture on the flowers turned the pollen into floral ink. As hard as they tried, they couldn't completely remove the stains.

. . . . .

My Advice: Quite often something that starts out so non--threatening and beautiful can quickly turn into a nightmare. This potential risk should be discussed with the florist. One florist told me that the stamens, which carry the pollen, should have been removed. Find out exactly what the hazards are with a particular flower, such as "Are these flowers prone to staining?" Do they contain anything toxic to humans or animals? Also, if staining does occur, are there any effective removers?

THE SPARKLING BRIDE

The bride and bridesmaids were doing their final hair and makeup touch-ups at the bride's house. One of the bridesmaids pulled out a

*bottle of skin lotion that had little sparkles in it. She started apply-
ing it on her skin. Once the other young women saw what she was
doing, they all put sparkling lotion on their skin. Whenever any of
them were photographed in bright sun or with an electronic flash,
little shiny white spots would appear on their skin.*

. . . . .

My Advice: The sparkles in the lotion caused the unexpected
reflections. The sparkles were in essence, micro mirrors, which
reflected light quite the same way a sequin on a dress would. It
turned into a photographer's nightmare because the little white
spots were very distracting. This in turn required extensive photo
retouching which I'm sure many photographers would not even
do! An innocent act blossomed into a bigger problem. Sometimes
it's better to forego a little glamour to avoid problems such as this.

THE REUNION

*The plan was for me to begin at the bride's house well before the
ceremony, to take some traditional family and wedding party photos. The bride's parents' home was gorgeous with a tiled foyer and
large staircase. This was the chosen location and the photo session
began as planned. A few minutes later, the front doorbell rang, and
some of the bride's old friends from college came in. They hugged and
exchanged pleasantries for several minutes, and then the photo session resumed. About ten minutes later the doorbell rang again. Same
story, it was more of the bride's friends that she hadn't seen in quite
some time. In the next fifteen minutes this happened twice more. The
only difference was that it was the bride's relatives that she hadn't*

seen in a long time. The cumulative effect of all these interruptions wasted at least thirty minutes of valuable time. The photo session ended abruptly because it was time to leave for the ceremony.

. . . . .

My Advice: There was clearly a conflict of interest at the bride's home. Whether the bride is just getting ready, or participating in a requested photo shoot, this is not the time to rendezvous with old acquaintances. This can be done a day or so earlier or at the reception. Whoever directed all the traffic to the bride's home wasn't thinking too clearly. This subsequently put a big time restraint on the activity the bride had planned.

THE WELL-GREASED BRIDE

The bride looked beautiful. She was dressed, on time and ready to go out the door. Her dad obliged and held the front storm door open to assist her departure. However, as she walked out, her dress dragged over the hydraulic storm door closer, leaving a big grease mark. The bride's dad felt terrible but the bride felt even worse and burst into tears.

. . . . .

My Advice: It's amazing how often this happens. Limos, car doors and church doors all have the potential for ruining the bride's gown. The maid of honor should assist the bride wherever she goes, especially going through doorways. By holding her train and folding the sides in, the bride and maid of honor should be able to carefully negotiate the narrowest of doorways without any problems.

THE WELL-GREASED FLOWER GIRL

You guessed it; if it can happen to the bride, it can happen to the flower girls or bridesmaids. The front door of the bride's home was opened and the storm door was closed. Someone said, "The limousines are here!" The flower girl ran over to look out the door and managed to get grease on her dress. Once again the culprit was the hydraulic storm door cylinder.

. . . . .

My Advice: Why not clean the front door thoroughly and then tape a paper towel or wrap a clean tee shirt over the cylinder? This will greatly reduce the chances of this happening and put your mind at ease.

THOSE DANGEROUS HEMLINES

One of the bridesmaids was running late. While hurrying to get out of her car, she caught her heel in the hemline of her dress. She fell on the ground, bruising her arm and tore a portion of her hemline. Fortunately, she wasn't too seriously hurt. So, with some quick emergency repairs to her dress, the show went on.

. . . . .

My Advice: The long hemlines can be quite hazardous when combined with high heels. If possible, have all the bridesmaids get ready at the same location. If this is not feasible, and a member of the group has a tendency to run late, tell them to be there an hour earlier, but don't tell them it's earlier. Be sure to have a sewing kit on hand to handle these emergencies. It's also a good idea for the bride and bridesmaids to scuff the bottom of their shoes early in the day to avoid slippery soles.

Dog Doo Won't Do!

The bride had a revered family dog that normally roamed and played freely on the family property. On the wedding day, the bride left through the front door of her home while the maid of honor was diligently holding the bride's train. On the way to the limo, the bride decided to take a shortcut across the front lawn. Unbeknownst to the bride, either her pet or a neighborhood dog had left droppings on her front lawn that she promptly walked through. Surprisingly the bride, being a fervent dog lover, literally took it all in stride. However, this delayed her departure because she sat on the edge of the limo seat while the unlucky maid of honor had the disgusting job of cleaning her shoes.

. . . . .

My Advice: The maid of honor, the bride's right hand woman, has a broad range of responsibility. The situation could have been much worse if her gown had been soiled. Even with the gown being held up, it's quite often difficult for the bride to see immediately in front of her feet. Stick to the walkway! Why not delegate a responsible adult to scout the area just before the bride leaves?

Panic in the Ranks

It was time for the bride and bridesmaids to leave her home and go to the church. The weatherman had predicted clearing weather but just as the bridal party was leaving, there was a torrential downpour. The limo driver provided a large golf umbrella and met the girls at the door. The bride's front staircase was quite narrow and made of concrete and brick. Several bridesmaids huddled under the umbrella as they made their exit.

While holding up their hemlines (which partially obstructed their view of the path) they tried to walk in unison with the umbrella and each other. In their haste, one of the bridesmaids slipped or missed a step and fell down hard on her arm and shoulder. This resulted in a big painful scrape but it could have been worse. Nothing was broken, so she didn't require any emergency treatment. Fortunately she was an athletic young woman, and with a few over the counter pain killers, she made it through the day.

· · · · ·

My Advice: Nothing will panic the bride and bridesmaids like bad weather. It's understandable that they will worry about their hair, makeup and clothes. Someone needs to step up, recognize potential dangers and take precautions. Here's where taking extra time and a brief pep talk can avoid trouble. This is what it might sound like: "Now ladies, don't worry about the rain, take your time, and walk slowly out to the limo. Pay attention to where you're walking and don't do anything hasty." Don't overcrowd the umbrella because the person on the perimeter who's getting wet will panic and be more prone to an accident.

CHAPTER 3

TRANSPORTATION

A BAFFLING MOMENT

The bride and groom were avid motorcyclists. The plan was to leave the church on a motorcycle and drive to a nearby restaurant for their wedding reception. The bride, wearing a traditional wedding gown, climbed on the motorcycle behind the groom. She then gathered her gown as best as she could and off they went. By the time she arrived at the banquet facility, her veil was in disarray and she had carbon from the exhaust pipe all over her gown.

. . . . .

My Advice: Wedding gowns and motorcycles are not a good mix. Her gown could have gotten caught in the wheels, causing a serious accident. Fortunately, this did not happen. Her gown however, did get covered with black exhaust soot. A bride on a motorcycle is a guarantee that the gown will get dirty. Reserve the motorcycle ride for going away when you're wearing appropriate clothing.

A CLASSIC SURPRISE

The bride and her mom looked into having an antique Rolls Royce for her wedding day. The limousine company they had contacted indicated that they just bought one and had it shipped over from England. The bride and her mom went to the limo company and saw photos of the company's new acquisition. The bride's mother wanted to surprise her daughter on her wedding day, so she pretended the idea of hiring a classic Rolls Royce was too expensive. The wedding day arrived and the bride's mom had the Rolls Royce waiting in order to surprise the bride and her husband after the ceremony. As the bride left the church, she was thrilled to see the Rolls Royce in front of the church. The newlyweds entered the classic car for their thirty minute ride to the reception hall. Five minutes into the ride, they realized that the interior of the car smelled like musty old upholstery. This wasn't the pleasant ride they expected. They couldn't wait to leave the car when they arrived at the reception.

. . . . .

My Advice: Quite often antique cars are stored for long periods of time in damp areas. This could be an unheated garage or the interior of a cargo ship. This usually leads to bad smelling upholstery. This is in no way a reflection of the make or model of the vehicle. This could happen to any car that has been stored improperly. In fact, I rather love photographing classic Rolls with their beautiful lines. When renting a classic ride for your wedding day, you should always ask to see the car in person. Ideally, a ten minute ride will give you a better idea exactly what you're getting yourself into. When the engine's running, is it making any strange sounds? Is the car putting out any puffs of black smoke or unusual smells? Is the vehicle equipped with air conditioning? Be aware of what you're getting because your comfort is at stake.

CRYING WOLF

The bride and bridesmaids were leaving her home through the front door when I asked them to look my way for a quick group photo. This would have taken a maximum of ten seconds. The limo _driver, not minding his own business, cried out, "You're gonna be late for church; there's no time for this!" This created a great deal of anxiety for the bride, the bridesmaids, and the bride's mom that was already standing outside. So instead of a relaxed, impromptu group photo, the entire group now looked stressed. They quickly loaded into the limo and left for the church. In addition, the route limo driver chose took them fifteen miles out of their way. This was not the most direct route to the ceremony, and consequently they were about ten minutes late._

Upon arriving at the church, the limo driver was true to his stress-creating form. While he held the door open for the girls, he exclaimed, "I saw the priest standing in the doorway, and he looked mad as hell!" This created an unbelievable amount of stress in this group. By now the mother of the bride's face was twitching with anxiety as they hurried inside.

. . . . .

My Advice: The limo driver, an older retired man, was marching to the beat of a different drummer. He caused problems every step of the way by making unsubstantiated claims based on conjecture. Instead of being a calming force, his unsolicited narration definitely created unnecessary anxiety. Not knowing the most direct route to the church further complicated the problem. Limo companies cover very large geographic areas, so it's virtually impossible to always know the best way to arrive at a particular destination. Be sure to ask the driver if he knows the most direct route to the church and if he's familiar with the area. If not, be sure to provide up to date, accurate directions. Try to find out who your limo driver will be ahead of time. Does he have a pleasant demeanor? Do your personalities agree or clash?

FANTASY ISLAND

The bride and groom planned a wedding on a beautiful resort island. It was early spring and the off season rates for the function hall and hotel looked inviting. The plan was for the guests to either fly to the island or take a ferry from the mainland. The big day arrived and the area was inundated with a heavy fog. This grounded all the airplanes at the local airports. The only alternative was the ferry but it was delayed until the fog lifted. When the ferry did depart later, it couldn't travel at the normal speed. A two and a half hour trip turned into four grueling hours. Many of the guests couldn't go out to the island a day early and ended up missing the actual wedding ceremony.

. . . . .

My Advice: Whenever a location wedding is planned, make sure you have plenty of options if something unexpected should occur. The ideal situation is to provide lodging a day ahead of time to insure that key people will be in attendance. Keep in mind that wedding service people, such as the photographer, videographer, florist, minister or officiator might have to be brought out to the island as well. This really depends on how remote the island is and what services are readily available.

FOILED BY ANTIQUITY

It was a winter wedding, and the plan was for the bride and her parents to ride to church in a classic antique car. The church was thirty five miles away, and they would follow the full size limousine

41

that was carrying the rest of the wedding party. Five minutes into the trip it started to snow heavily, which was unusual this early in the season. Most limo companies store their classic cars to protect them during the winter. For some reason, this company did not. The windshield wipers in this classic ride were vacuum wipers, meaning they were not controlled by an electric motor (see Glossary). Every time the antique car would stop, the wipers would also stop. This was standard equipment on vehicles manufactured between 1920 and 1960. It resulted in very poor visibility because the wipers couldn't maintain a constant speed. For this reason the classic ride had to travel at a much slower speed than a modern limousine. Needless to say, the bride and her parents arrived at church about a half hour later than the rest of the wedding party.

. . . . .

My Advice: Once the wedding day starts to run late, it's very difficult to make up for lost time. You'll hear this often because it's true and important. This problem could have happened to anyone riding in any antique car without electric wipers. It could also have happened in heavy rain. Make sure you find out ahead of time how your transportation will fare under extenuating weather circumstances.

GET ME TO THE CHURCH ON TIME

The limousine was right on time. It pulled up in front of the bride's home one hour before the ceremony. It was a comfortable day so the driver opened the windows and shut off the engine. A half hour later, the bride and bridesmaids came out of the house, and entered the limo. The driver entered the limo and tried to start the engine repeatedly, but the engine would not start. Normally, they would be enough privately owned cars at the bride's house to accommodate the bride, her parents and the bridesmaids. However, at this particular wedding, the husbands and boyfriends dropped off their dates with the intention of meeting them later at the reception after the limo had finished for the day. With few alternatives and no time to waste, I offered the use of my minivan. The bride accepted and she and the bridesmaids promptly climbed into my van. Some people had to sit on others' laps. The van became the emergency limousine and the women arrived on time for the ceremony.

. . . . .

My Advice: Always have an alternate plan in place. Fortunately, there was an emergency solution. A last minute breakdown doesn't allow time for the limousine company to send out for a replacement car.

I CAN'T GO THERE!

The bride's dad owned a well-established nursery and landscape business. So when he found out his daughter was getting married, he planted an elaborate garden right in front of his house. The plan was for the wedding party photos to be taken there. After the ceremony was over, the wedding party entered the stretch limousine. When they approached the bride's home, the limo driver said, "I can't drive up that steep hill. I'll bottom out!" All the bride's father's hard work was for nothing and the photo session took place elsewhere.

. . . . .

My Advice: The bride's house was at the top of a long, narrow steep hill. In this era of stretch limousines, no one considered that the car couldn't physically negotiate the hill. It would have been like a boat getting grounded on a sand bar. When the wedding party was offered the opportunity to walk up the hill, they all declined. They were all really disgruntled with the limo driver, but whose fault was it?

I HAVE TO CLEAN THE LIMO!

The bride had hired the limo for four hours. After about three and a half hours, the limo driver started to put pressure on the people who hired him. He stated, "I have to drop you off now. I have another wedding to go to and I still have to go back to the shop and clean the limo!"

. . . . .

My Advice: Many times, limousine companies will overbook their schedule. This is more characteristic of a small company during the height of the wedding season. When you retain the services of a limo company, make sure the hours they'll be working for you are clearly defined. Cleaning the limo and preparing for their next job should not be done in your designated time frame.

JUST KEEP UP

The bride gave key wedding day professionals, explicit directions to get to her home and the church. However, she didn't know exactly how to get from the church to the reception's location. This was an exclusive restaurant in a big city rife with large, ongoing construction projects. She told me and the other hired help, "Just follow the limousines to the restaurant!" After the church ceremony, I approached the limo driver and said, "I'll be following you to the reception, so if you can keep me in your rear view mirror, I'd appreciate it!" The limo driver lacked a friendly demeanor and rudely said, "You'll just have to keep up!"

So after a frantic high speed drive, the limo entered the city. The city was loaded with one way streets, detours and street lights. Needless to say, the limo lost the key wedding help at a red light just a few blocks from the banquet destination. It seems there was a local shortcut to approach the hotel/banquet facility. It took some time to ask for directions, to figure where to go and where to park. Consequently, I didn't arrive at the same time as the wedding party but arrived twenty minutes later.

. . . . .

My Advice: Whenever there's a lot of traveling associated with a wedding, it's very important to give complete, explicit directions to all parties concerned. This includes all the guests, relatives and all the hired help. The information must be current and include all stops on the way. In this era of online map searching, one must check the accuracy of the map and the directions. GPS devices don't always work near tall buildings or during bad weather. You must also consider if there are any events, parades, festivals, detours or construction that may impact the directions. You must give this the serious attention it deserves beforehand to avoid problems on the big day.

REARING TO GO

The bride had booked a horse and carriage to tour a large city just prior to her wedding ceremony. Accompanying her were her parents and the maid of honor. I sat up front with the carriage driver in order to photograph the excursion. The other four passengers sat on the two rear seats. After touring the city for about an hour, the driver parked the carriage about two blocks from where the bride was getting married. It was still about fifteen minutes too early to drop the bride off. The driver leaned the reins over the front seat and disembarked. Within ten seconds, a leaf blew down the street and spooked the horse. It reared out of control. The carriage shook and jostled to the point that it was going to tip over or take off without the driver. Needless to say, this scared the hell out of everyone. I quickly grabbed the reins and pulled back. This ended the animal's revolt and a dangerous situation was averted.

. . . . .

My Advice: Was the driver negligent? Should the reins have been secured? Yes! Animals are very unpredictable. This could have turned out badly for all parties concerned; fortunately it didn't. When hiring horses and buggies for your wedding day, be sure to ask what controls are in place? Should the driver ever leave the horse unattended? What measures could be taken in emergency situations?

SPREAD OUT WEDDING

It was a cold, winter night in Boston. In fact, it was a Friday night during the busiest holiday season of the year. The church ceremony had just ended and the bride and groom had requested a photo session in the church because it was very dark and cold outside. This was done very quickly and then the wedding party climbed into the limo. The reception was in a hotel in Providence, at least fifty-five miles away. This didn't bother the wedding party as they broke out champagne and beer. Their celebration had begun. Traffic was very heavy on their way out of town. The highway wasn't much better. Visibility was extremely poor and driving was quite challenging and hazardous to say the least. After about an hour, the majority of the guests had arrived but not the wedding party.

After another half hour elapsed, the wedding party finally arrived. It seems that they had to make a few stops on the way for those who needed a bathroom break. When they finally disembarked, they still had to bring in all their luggage and check into the hotel before the reception could begin. The wedding party numbered about twenty-four people, so checking in took an eternity. This added another fifty minutes to their tardiness. Needless to say, the wedding reception started extremely late.

· · · · ·

My Advice: How practical was this planning? This was a situation that was destined for problems even before it began. By selecting a church closer to the hotel or by selecting a function hall closer to the church, they would have saved at least an hour. The celebration that took place in the limo only precipitated more stops for the driver. The large wedding party checking in at the hotel all at the same time in an inebriated state, only made the process more tedious. The unfortunate wedding guests waited for what seemed like an eternity for the real celebration to begin. Someone obviously didn't consider all the consequences of this plan.

THE BIG SQUEEZE

The groom had hired three limousines to accommodate his large family and the wedding party. The ceremony had ended and the limos with all the occupants arrived at the designated location. The place where family and wedding party photos were to be taken was a private garden that allowed the use of their grounds for a substantial fee. Twenty minutes into the session, the limo drivers said they couldn't stick around much longer because they had another event to go to.

The groom was furious because he was under the impression that he had all three limos for at least another two hours. There seemed to be some sort of misunderstanding about the actual time they were to begin and end their services. Here was a large group of people who needed a way to get to the function hall which was about eight miles away but they weren't ready to leave yet. This posed quite a dilemma for the groom. He thought he had everything under control. After a little negotiating with the limo drivers, they reached a compromise. One of the limos would stay to shuttle people back to the reception and the other two would leave.

. . . . .

My Advice: This type of scenario happens quite often. Limousine companies have a tendency to overbook during the height of the wedding season. Sometimes they will offer to start a little earlier so they can finish a little earlier. This rarely works out because the bride is going to be ready at a certain time according to her schedule. All the subsequent appointments and events would have to be rearranged. You definitely don't want to lose your primary mode of transportation earlier than expected. You must have the limousines' schedule confirmed in writing when you book their services. This must also be reconfirmed prior to the wedding day.

THE LIMO MARATHON NIGHTMARE

The bride had a very large wedding party so she hired two stretch limos and an antique car. When the driver of the classic car arrived, he was surprised to find out that the church ceremony was taking place at a country church about fifty miles away. He assumed it was a local church with the same name and neglected to ask the bride in what city the church was located. The entourage of the three vehicles left for their long journey. One of the groomsmen didn't want to ride back from the function hall in the limo but wanted to drive his own car. So, one of the limos and the antique car proceeded directly to the out of town church. The other limo proceeded to the reception to pick up the groomsman who was dropping off his beloved car.

The function hall was situated about twenty miles from the church and the drive consisted of country roads. The classic car

49

and one limo arrived at church right on time. The other limo that had to make a stop on the way was nowhere to be found. It was time for the ceremony to begin, but only the bride, groom and half the wedding party were there. A call was made to the other driver as to his whereabouts. It seems that the other limo became lost on the poorly marked, curvy country roads and was trying to regain his bearings. There was nothing to do except wait for the other limo to arrive. The incomplete wedding party waited in the back of the church. The two drivers went to a fast food restaurant directly across from the church. From there, they ate their lunch and kept their eyes on their unlocked cars.

A short while later, a suspicious acting man opened the limo doors and helped himself to whatever he could get his hands on. This turned out to be the driver's attaché case with personal papers and his cell phone. Fortunately, the bridesmaid's pocketbooks were locked up in the trunk. The drivers gave chase and followed the man to a housing project not far away. They decided to call the police to report the crime. To add to the confusion, the police arrived at the same time as the missing limo. The second limo was over one hour late. The officiating priest and all the guests were totally perplexed by this unnecessary delay. The ceremony began and proceeded at a ridiculously fast pace. The ceremony ended as swiftly as it had begun. The wedding party exited the church to witness the local police department buzzing all over the crime scene and driving up and down the local streets looking for the suspect. This surreal scene looked like a television police drama.

The wedding party entered the limos as quickly as they could and proceeded to the country restaurant. The food at the banquet facility was ready to serve so introductions were made hurriedly. The meal was served at a breakneck speed. The reception was now limited to a two hour event because another function was slated for later that day. All the typical wedding day activities were done in an abbreviated fashion. The stressful celebration ended abruptly.

. . . . .

My Advice: One must pay attention to all the details of the wedding day. The groomsman who had insisted he drop off his car at the function hall for purely selfish reasons created a time delay nightmare that snowballed into a fiasco. As I mentioned earlier, once an event starts to run late, it's nearly impossible to make up for lost time. The bride should have insisted that the groomsman stick to the game plan and delegate someone else to drop off the car. The limo drivers should have locked their doors as no one never really knows when a thief may strike. Create a schedule, make sure everyone involved knows all the details, and at all costs try to stick with the plan.

THE LOCKOUT

It started out as a beautiful, hot August day. A brand new, pearlescent ivory stretch limousine pulled up in front of the bride's house. The driver was right on time. The ceremony was to begin in twenty minutes and the bride lived only five minutes away. The limo driver cranked up the air conditioning and jumped out to assist the bride and wedding party. He then tried to open the door for the bride and much to his chagrin, he realized that his only set of keys were still in the ignition and everyone was locked out. Panic set in as the limo driver frantically tried opening the other doors, but to no avail. They were all locked. It was time for the bride and bridesmaids to leave for the ceremony. A desperate call was made to the home office of the limo company requesting a second key. They dispatched someone right away, but they were situated forty-five minutes away from the bride's house and they had to contend with Friday afternoon rush traffic.

Meanwhile the limo driver, trying to be resourceful, requested a wire coat hanger from the bride. After straightening the hanger out, he then tried to access the lock mechanism through the top of the closed windows and the edge of the door. Both were quite formidable. I suggested that they try the rear upper hatch window because it was not surrounded in metal and looked like it had a little more give. The limo driver and I both tugged on the bottom of the upper tailgate and it showed a little more promise. There was a lock release mechanism situated in the rear of the limo, not far from the tailgate. The coat hanger still didn't work, and the deep tinted windows didn't help either as you couldn't see what you were doing through the glass.

I suggested that a bridesmaid with slim arms stick her hand through the small opening created while the limo driver and I tugged at the bottom of the window. A volunteer bridesmaid stepped forward and an attempt was made but she couldn't quite reach the lock mechanism. Tension was building by the minute. What happened next was a nightmare. The two year old ring bearer, whose mom was a bridesmaid, fell off the sidewalk and rolled under the limo. Of course the engine was still running, and coincidentally, the limo was parked on a hill. His mom quickly grabbed him by his tuxedo lapels and quickly pulled him to safety. She simultaneously released a flurry of profanities directed at the limo driver. This heightened the stress considerably.

The limo driver knew he had messed up and was doing the best he could to remedy the situation. I suggested that if the bridesmaid held some scissors in her hand while reaching in the rear tailgate, she may be able to reach the lock mechanism. Someone brought out scissors and an attempt was made to reach the lock as the limo driver and I pulled up on the upper tailgate.

It took the combined strength of both of us to pull on the thick window glass to allow just enough room for the bridesmaid to get her hand under the glass. Reaching out with the scissors, the lock made a clicking sound. The limo driver, hearing the sound, immediately let go of the window to check the side door to see if it was unlocked. With only me holding the upper tailgate, the window acted as a spring loaded mousetrap, trapping the bridesmaid's hand beneath the window. She yelled in distress and the limo driver quickly returned after realizing he left his task too soon and the doors were still locked.

Another attempt was made to unlock the door. This time, I implored the limo driver not to run away if he heard a click and we focused all our strength and energy on the task at hand. We pulled on the upper tailgate, the bridesmaid stretched to the limit, and an actual click was heard. Someone tried the door and it opened. The bride, bridesmaids, and ring bearer quickly jumped in after twenty minutes of pure hysteria. The limo driver pulled up to the church only ten minutes late. The limo driver was somewhat exonerated.

· · · · ·

My Advice: Whether the limo driver accidentally locked the doors when he was getting out of the auto or the wind blew the door shut is inconsequential. This scenario could have happened to anyone. The limousine driver wasn't the most popular guy that day. This could have been avoided by having a spare key in the driver's wallet or hiding one under the limo in a magnetic key case. Why not ask the limo company if they have a contingency plan for such occurrences?

THE ONE HORSE RIDE

The bride hired a horse and buggy for her wedding day. The plan was to take the bride from her home to the church. Then after the church, the buggy would take them to the restaurant. What would have been a ten minute car ride, took at least forty-five minutes by horse power. The ride consisted of narrow city streets. After the ceremony, their ride to the function hall took another forty-five minutes. This was a big waste of time and the guests had to wait at the church and again at the function hall.

. . . . .

My Advice: I'm sure many brides perceive a horse and buggy as a romantic novelty. What they often overlook is that horse and buggy transportation is SLOW! Unless you live in close proximity to where you're going, or have a lot of time to waste, carefully consider this option. Horses can be very crude and unpredictable. Anything they can do in a barn or in a field, they can do on your wedding day.

THE HORSE RAN OUT OF GAS

It was a beautiful, hot, sunny summer day. The church ceremony was over and the bride and groom entered a small horse drawn buggy that would take them nine miles to the wedding reception. It started out as a fun ride, up and down hills, out of the city and into the country.

About halfway to their destination, the horse started to slow down and show signs of sweating, moderately at first and profusely shortly thereafter. Five minutes later, he started frothing at the mouth. The driver knew it was time to pull over, remove his harness and rescue him from his arduous task. A limo was called to pick up the newlyweds and a trailer called to pick up the horse and buggy.

. . . . .

My Advice: Was it simply too hot for the horse or was he just too old? Who knows? In the previous story, we established that horses can be a slow means of transportation. This story shows that horses are unpredictable. If you have plenty of extra time on your wedding day, then you might want to hire a horse and buggy. If not, go with a sure means of dependable transportation.

THE PUSHY DRIVER

It was a sweltering hot summer day when the stretch limousine arrived at a scenic park. This was the location that the bride and groom had selected for group and family photos. Everyone disembarked from the limo when the driver suggested to the groomsmen, "Why don't you take off your jackets?" The groomsmen responded collectively," No it's OK, we'll keep them on!" The driver replied," Well, don't blame me if you feel faint. I work as a nurse during the week. I've been driving a limo for thirteen years so I know what I'm talking about. Why don't you sit in the limo? This tirade of bumptious dialogue continued right through the photo session. "Why don't you take pictures over there?" Why don't you do this? Why don't you do that? I finally said to the driver, "Why don't you let me do my job? I've been doing this for thirty years and that's what I'm getting paid for."

. . . . .

My Advice: Quite often, while attempting to be helpful, limo drivers will overstep their boundaries. This is not all that uncommon for someone familiar with one aspect of the wedding day, to deem themselves self-appointed experts in many fields. Every wedding related professional has a job to do. When the hired help crosses over into someone else's realm, it's the responsibility of whoever hired them to politely intercede.

THE TOO LARGE LIMO

The bride and groom had a very large wedding party, so they hired the largest limo they could find. The bride lived in a city with narrow streets and small city blocks, so when the limo arrived, it occupied half a city block when parked. The entire wedding party entered the limo and started off to the church ceremony. They had no sooner arrived at the end of the street when their first problem occurred. The limo could hardly negotiate the small inner city intersections. Each ninety degree turn took several attempts of inching forward and backing up, inching forward and backing up. This turned what should have been a pleasant ride to church into an aggravating situation. It also considerably delayed the arrival time.

. . . . .

My Advice: The novelty of having the biggest limo available clearly overshadowed its practicality. No one considered the ramifications of an extremely large limo vs. the small narrow streets. The wedding party would have been much better off riding in two smaller limos than one giant limo. When details are overlooked, problems occur.

THE WINDSWEPT BRIDE

It was a beautiful warm summer night and the bride planned on riding to the church in her grandfather's antique car. The classic convertible was restored to showroom condition. Due to the warm weather, the convertible top was down. The front seat was designated for the bride's parents while the bride would ride alone in the back. Her large dress and veil needed more room than the front seat could provide. The church was only about five miles from the bride's home and they all looked forward to a relaxing ride in a country setting. Grandpa was acting as the chauffeur. Once everyone was aboard, they embarked on their journey. Shortly thereafter, they realized their dilemma. Even at twenty-five miles per hour, there was quite a breeze whipping across the back seat. The bride's veil threatened to blow off. Her styled hair seemed to be in jeopardy as well. They didn't have time to stop and put up the top, as the ceremony was to begin shortly. So she ducked her head down and assumed the lowest profile she possibly could. An enjoyable ride suddenly turned into a nightmare.

. . . . .

My Advice: Quite often the bride has her hair and veil done before her wedding day. This is a test so she can determine if she really wants that style for her wedding day. Perhaps a ride in Grandpa's antique car on that very same day would be helpful. This would let everyone know what to expect with the top down. She could also find out if her bridal veil would fit with the top up. No one considered the consequences of riding in the backseat of a convertible.

WHERE'S THE LIMOUSINE?

The limousine was late and the bride was furious. If there was a problem she should have at least received a phone call. As it turned out, the stretch limousine was stopped at a stop sign a few miles from the bride's house. A truck driver backed out of his driveway without looking and backed right into the middle of the limo. He broadsided the limo and bent it like a boomerang. When the driver tried to call the bride on his cell phone the battery died. He couldn't leave the scene of the accident to find a phone. A neighbor called the police. It wasn't until the police arrived that the driver was able to call the bride and a backup limo. In addition to this, accident information had to be exchanged.

. . . . .

My Advice: In this era of cell phones, any limo company should have more than one phone for emergency use. It's also wise to discuss a backup plan if anything happens to the primary means of transportation. A master list of all the key wedding personnel with their contact info, email addresses and cell phones is usually quite helpful. When all the key people receive the list before the wedding day, most problems that arise can be quickly resolved.

CHAPTER 4

THE CEREMONY

STAGE FRIGHT

The church was filled to its capacity with friends and relatives. The music was playing and the processional began. The wedding party proceeded down the aisle and took their positions at the front of the church. The music changed to Mendelssohn's "Wedding March", all heads turned to watch the bride walk down the aisle but no bride could be seen. The music continued to play but the bride still didn't show up.

As the photographer hired to photograph this event, I walked through a set of double doors in the rear of the church to see what was going on. Much to my surprise I witnessed a terrified bride pleading with her dad, "No, I can't do this. I can't walk down that aisle!" Her dad replied, "Oh yes, you're going down that aisle if I have to drag you!" She repeated her plea, "No, no, I can't do this!" This went on for several minutes. Finally her dad said, "Look, I've spent lots of money on this wedding and we can't cancel it now. So you're going down that aisle!"

I went back into the church and waited in the rear. Sure enough, a few minutes later dad and the bride appeared. The young bride was crying hysterically. She clung to her dad's arm like a drowning swimmer clinging to a life preserver. Despite her extreme anxiety and emotional meltdown, she made it to the front of the church. Once the ceremony began, she seemed a little better.

. . . . .

My Advice: The bride was just out of high school and extremely shy. When she first looked down the aisle and saw all the eyes focused on her, she tried to run away. Perhaps she suffered from agoraphobia, which is an abnormal fear of being in public places. All the attention caused her to emotionally break down. It was obvious she wasn't accustomed to public scrutiny. Maybe she would have felt more comfortable participating in a small, private ceremony and not a large church filled with people. If this sounds like something that might give you a problem, by all means seek an alternate solution. Psychological counseling with the appropriate anti-anxiety medication might help. You could elope or decide on a small, private ceremony with the immediate families. It's simply not worth the drama and the emotional meltdown to inflict such pain and discomfort on yourself.

WHERE'S GRANDMA?

Everyone was patiently waiting at the church for the ceremony to begin. The bride didn't want to start the ceremony until her grandmother arrived. She finally arrived about twenty-five minutes late. Apparently, she didn't know her way from the hotel to the church.

. . . . .

My Advice: Directions, directions, directions -- I can't say this enough. Be sure everyone (especially the principals) and your guests, know exactly where they're going. Print up directions with the appropriate telephone numbers and include this with your invitations. Be wary of those who might need a special set of directions. Confirm the accuracy of your directions. If you're not good at directions, delegate someone who is. Even maps and directions that are downloaded from the internet are sometimes flawed. They don't always take into account, recent road construction, detours, or civic events that might impact a route of travel. Finally, make sure that all elderly people have rides with those who are familiar with the area.

A THUNDEROUS APPLAUSE

It was a beautiful summer day and a late afternoon wedding was planned on a fifty acre private estate. A majestic pine grove near a lake was the chosen location for the ceremony. The plan was for all the guests to be shuttled from the main farm house to the pine grove via horse and buggy with the last arrival being the bride and her dad. The bride was to be married on the family's homestead. On one side of the alcove, a harpist played classical music. Everyone gazed down the dirt road in anticipation of the bride's arrival. The sound of hoof beats grew louder and the carriage came into view.

The carriage stopped at the edge of the path. The driver disembarked and unrolled a long red carpet. The bride's dad was the first to get out and then he helped his daughter. The musician played a traditional wedding march as the bride proceeded down the carpet to meet the groom. The harpist stopped playing. It was absolutely silent. I actually heard a pine cone fall from a tree. The ceremony began and the minister asked the groom, "Do you take this woman to be your lawfully wedded wife, to have and to hold, to love and cherish from this day forward until death do you part?"

Before the groom could answer, the tranquility of the moment was disturbed. The horse backfired (expelled gas) with *a thunderous blast and impeccable timing. The coachman jiggled the reins in hopes of disguising the disturbance but everyone knew what had happened. Judging by his cranberry red face, he knew it was a losing proposition. The guests laughed uncontrollably. After a brief pause that seemed like an eternity, the groom responded, "I do!"*

. . . . .

My Advice: Hindsight is always 20/20. The horse should have been moved to a different location beyond earshot during the ceremony. Whenever animals are involved in wedding ceremonies, anything can and will happen.

DAD CAN MAKE IT

The groom's dad was a diabetic and was in the hospital at the time the wedding was to take place. The groom and his siblings wanted dad to attend the wedding and be included in the family photos. The consensus of the family was that they thought everything would be okay. It was a warm spring day, and they figured the fresh air would do him some good. They picked him up from the hospital and brought him into church. During the ceremony he sat in his pew, looking pale as a ghost. The plan was to take him for family photos right after the ceremony was over and then take him right back to the hospital. The photo session was quickly organized.

I worked as fast as possible to accommodate the family's requests. The groom's dad was sitting down and looked like he was going to pass out at any minute. The photo session was quickly _terminated and 911 was called. An ambulance arrived and brought him back to the hospital._

. . . . .

My Advice: Sometimes wishful thinking can get you in trouble. The groom and his siblings wanted their dad to be present at this wedding. They totally forgot about his well-being. Taking him out of his hospital bed in a compromised state proved to be too much. Key decision makers must take a critical look at any medical situation. Consult the doctor in charge and act accordingly. "Oh, he'll be okay for just a couple of hours" just doesn't hold true when someone's life may be in jeopardy. Evaluate the situation carefully and act prudently. The smart thing to do would have been to leave dad in the hospital and have the family photos taken at his bedside.

Don't Leave Without Me!

The wedding ceremony and banquet reception was scheduled for a large, luxurious ferry. This boat would typically cruise to a scenic location and then the ceremony would proceed on deck, followed by the reception. The invitations read, "Please be at the docks no later than 1:30 PM, as the ferry will leave promptly at 2 PM." At 1:55 the bride received a call from one of her guests saying, "I had a flat tire and I'm still about a half hour away. Please don't leave without me!" The bride and her parents expressed their sympathies but reiterated that the ferry must *leave on time because they signed a contract that clearly stated a departure time and a return time so waiting for delayed guests was out of the question.*

. . . . .

My Advice: This was a tough situation for all parties concerned. Some people, however, are notoriously late. Should two hundred people be inconvenienced for the sake of a few? Wedding schedules have to be met. Food has to be prepared and served on time. Bands and disc jockeys are all retained for certain time limits. Typically a boat wedding has strict time restraints, especially when multiple commitments may already be on the books. Know your risks and discuss alternate plans!

DON'T MUDDY THE MOMENT!

This story is a great example of anticipating a problem and dealing with it before the wedding. The ceremony was planned outdoors in a gazebo. The bride would walk up a center aisle that was created by two groups of chairs. The grassy area had a tendency to be damp because it was located near a pond. Some water from the pond leached into the ground. Even in the middle of summer this was a soggy location. The bride's dad, who was in the construction business, built a series of plywood panels with decorative stenciling along the edges. This eliminated the bride's fear of muddying her gown.

. . . . .

My Advice: Carpets sold by florists don't work well in damp outdoor venues. Not every bride has the luxury of having dad build a plywood ramp. This was a great job of anticipating a problem and solving it. The banquet facility thought so too. They bought the ramp at the end of the day. A good alternative to that would be to rent a long carpet with rubber backing and roll it out only for the bride.

DYEING FOR THE DAY

The bride and bridesmaids wanted a certain shade of purple to go with the bridesmaids gowns. They couldn't find exactly what they were looking for. They bought white shoes and dyed them purple. There was a lot of buzz that day about how pleased they all were with the dyed results. Well it just so happened that it was an outdoor ceremony and it had rained earlier in the day. When the bridesmaids walked in the wet grass, their feet became wet. Before too long, the dye on their shoes started to run. They all ended up with purple feet. As soon as the outdoor ceremony ended, they all removed their shoes for fear of transferring the dye to the bottom of their dresses. So they spent the rest of the day barefoot.

· · · · ·

My Advice: When dealing with shoe dye, consult a professional in the field. It seems a final coat of waterproof sealer was missing from their plans and a disaster followed.

EMOTIONS IN CONTROL

The bride had selected a gown with a lengthy train and a veil to match. Every time the bride moved during the church ceremony her train and veil moved as well. As the ceremony ensued, the back side of her dress became more and more disheveled. The maid of honor was crying uncontrollably and was so engrossed in the ceremony, she neglected to tidy up the bride's gown. So throughout the ceremony, the bride's train lay in a crumpled heap, only to be recorded on video and still photography for years to come.

. . . . .

My Advice: This is actually a common occurrence. The maid of honor should be reminded of her duty prior to the ceremony, before she becomes an emotional wreck. She can't be so distracted that she can't manage the bride's gown, veil and maybe a few tissues. It would have been great to just yell out, "Hey, fix the gown!" but of course this would have been highly disruptive. Only someone standing nearby could save the moment with a whisper.

FOILED BY THE RUNNER

The wedding party was lined up at the rear of the church. It was moments before the bride and the wedding party would proceed down the aisle. Two of the groomsmen walked to the front of the church and unrolled a white runner. This can be made of flimsy plastic or fabric and is usually provided by the florist. The processional began with each bridesmaid being escorted down the aisle by the matching groomsman. The bridesmaids all wore spiked heels. It didn't take very long for their heels to catch and tear big holes in the runner. By the time the bride came down the aisle, the runner was ripped in at least two places. It was twisted and tangled into a deplorable mess. Instead of adding an element of elegance to the ceremony, it became an unsightly hazard.

. . . . .

My Advice: This particular aisle runner was the equivalent of a decorative paper towel. Were the bridesmaids' heels too pointy, or was the runner of extremely poor quality? Elegance went out the window and was replaced by a trip and fall hazard. Discuss this potential problem with your florist to avoid this unpleasant situation.

GLOVED BUT STILL LOVED

The bride wore long gloves that went up to her elbows. The ceremony was underway and it was time for the exchange of rings. It was a hot day and the bride's tight fitting gloves could not be removed. The groom did the only thing he could do, he placed the ring over his wife's glove. This only fit over the very tip of her finger. She wore it that way until the situation could be rectified.

. . . . .

My Advice: Whether her hands were sweaty or swollen, the gloves could not be easily removed. A common solution to this problem is to have the ring finger of the bride's left glove cut off and hemmed. This is usually done by the bridal salon when the gown is being altered. This way, only the finger is removed and not the entire glove.

HARSH LIGHT

The ceremony was taking place on the back of a large boat in the middle of the day. Everyone was lined up and the justice of the peace began the ceremony. The sun was intense and the entire wedding party stood in direct sunlight. This caused everyone to squint horribly. The harsh shadows on their faces didn't help the photography or the videography.

. . . . .

My Advice: This type of harsh lighting is commonly referred to as hatchet lighting. It destroys facial characteristics with heavy shadows. Even if the entire wedding party wore sunglasses, the overall scene would be fractured by extreme highlights and very dark shadows. A shaded area, a canopy or something to take the wedding party out of intense sunlight would be in order. You should also consider the comfort factor for the people being blinded.

It Took Guts to Wear Tails

The groom and groomsmen arrived at church well before the ceremony. The groomsmen wore black regular length tuxedos and the groom wore tails with a jacket cut short in the front at the waist. His outfit was reminiscent of a concert pianist. The groom was a large man, well over six feet tall. He must have been an avid eater or a beer drinker because his pot belly protruded from his tuxedo. This unsightly characteristic was most obvious during the vows and ring exchange when both the bride and groom were in profile. This created problems for me as well as the videographer, trying to hide this unflattering feature.

. . . . .

My Advice: What was the tuxedo shop thinking? They should have provided a little more guidance to the groom. His outfit should have hidden his physical flaws and not accentuated them. Maybe the bride should have gone to the tuxedo shop with the groom to make sure everything looked okay. An impartial third party opinion can sometimes go a long way in averting a disaster.

Justice of the Peace for a Day

In some states, an individual can get a one day license to act as a justice of the peace. This would allow a friend or relative of the bride or groom to legally marry them. One of the groom's friends had offered to do exactly that. The wedding day arrived and the ceremony began. He struggled through the entire ceremony. He pronounced them "man and wife" and neglected to have them exchange rings. The entire ceremony was unscripted and flawed.

. . . . .

My Advice: Why not leave the officiating to the professionals? An actual justice of the peace is not that expensive. They usually can only charge a fee that's predetermined by the state in which they're licensed. This one time justice of the peace clearly needed rehearsal time and an outline on an index card for guidance.

No License, No Marriage

The wedding party rushed to get to church on time. The minister had warned them not to be late. In their haste, they forgot the wedding license at home. The minister informed them that he could not marry them without the license in hand. This created an emergency situation with all the guests in church and the ceremony about to begin. After a brief discussion, a compromise was reached. Someone was sent back to the house to get the license while the minister started the buildup to the actual ceremony. A key member of the family, who was not a member of the wedding party, was elected for the task. The ceremony began. When the carrier returned with the wedding license, they paused the ceremony and everyone cheered.

. . . . .

My Advice: Checklists are very important. Wedding day haste can easily lead to something being forgotten somewhere. Create a checklist during a quiet moment well before your wedding day and make use of it!

No Photos Allowed!

The bride and groom selected a scenic location that was run by the local historical society. The grounds consisted of an old estate with a barn. The barn had been renovated to accommodate banquets. The ceremony would be outside in the garden area. The plan was for the photographer to arrive one hour early to individually photograph the bride's and groom's families. All the key people arrived one hour early when they were immediately approached by the property manager. He immediately announced, "We don't permit photos to be taken until the actual ceremony begins!" This was a complete shock to the bride and groom. This was never explained to them when they were paying their deposit.

. . . . .

My Advice: This was a totally arbitrary rule because the photos would be taken outside, not within the confines of any precious indoor space. In addition to this, the property was not very well kept. The area where the ceremony was taking place was surrounded with low hanging branches which were inundated by large spider webs. The barn where the banquet was located had only one antiquated restroom to accommodate all the guests. Find out what you're actually getting when reserving a location. Ask all the appropriate questions. Visit the grounds in daylight when you can roam around the property. Ask if there are any restrictions on its use.

OFF TO THE RACES

The ceremony was taking place in one of the oldest historical churches in North America. It was a night wedding, and as in many very old churches, it was very dimly lit. That's because candles and lanterns were all that were available when the church was built. When electricity was added at a later date, it was done to minimize structural damage. It was also done very inconspicuously, to maintain the historical integrity of the building. The mother of the groom specifically asked me to take a photo of everyone coming down the aisle during the processional. This is normally, not a problem at all. However, at this particular church, which was a national historic monument, flash photography was NOT permitted under any circumstances. This meant that everything had to be photographed on a tripod with very slow shutter speeds. I discussed this with the groom's mom, and explained that everyone would have to walk very slowly to accomplish this objective. I also asked that she brief the wedding party on this requirement because they were in isolation and I wouldn't have the opportunity to speak with them in person. The processional began and the wedding party raced down the very short, dimly lit aisle at an extremely fast pace. This caused the photos to look soft and blurry.

. . . . .

My Advice: Don't ask or expect the impossible. Photography is based on concrete set of physical requirements. When special requests are made, cooperation is essential. The mother of the groom obviously didn't communicate very well or not at all with the wedding party. Granted, with the advent of digital photography, low light levels are a little more manageable. However, nothing can compensate for subjects moving too fast for the existing lighting conditions.

SILENT CEREMONY

The ceremony was taking place in a gazebo situated in a beautiful outdoor garden. The minister who was officiating discussed and reviewed the basic sequence of events with the principals. He also received instructions on operating the microphone. Fifteen feet in front of the gazebo were two sections of chairs, twenty rows deep and fifteen chairs wide. This arrangement formed a center aisle. The ceremony began and the wedding party proceeded down the aisle. The minister stood in the gazebo, facing the crowd in front of the couple he was about to marry. He greeted all the guests and then started the ceremony. Ten minutes into his speech he asked "Will all present bear witness to this event?" The response was almost nonexistent. He then said, "That was a pretty poor response!" and someone in the crowd yelled, "Why don't you turn on the microphone?" He blushed in embarrassment, turned it on and repeated the question. They then responded with a resounding, "We will!" Fortunately, this was before the wedding vows and exchange of rings, so the guests could follow along with the ceremony.

. . . . .

My Advice: Despite repeated subtle attempts to quietly tell the minister to turn on the microphone so the spectators could hear, he didn't do it. No one wanted to interrupt the ceremony by yelling "Turn on the microphone!" Sometimes this is the only solution. When you consider the effects of the ceremony only being heard by a few people in the front rows vs. the entire audience, shouting out isn't so bad after all. Perhaps a note taped to the microphone might have corrected the situation a little sooner. How about asking the minister to question the crowd, "Can you hear me back there?"

SPRING SHOWERS

It was a beautiful spring day and a very large wedding party of about twenty-four people had just processed down the aisle. The ceremony was underway. Five minutes before the ceremony ended, the skies opened up with strong thunderstorms. The ceremony finished and it was still raining heavily. Not wanting to go outside, the maid of honor suggested, "Why don't we take some group photos in the church?" This seemed like a great idea. Before anyone could answer, she immediately led the wedding party up the side aisle to the front of the church. The priest, who was still cleaning up after the ceremony snarled in a most annoyed tone of voice, "What do you think you're doing?" The maid of honor replied," We're hoping to take pictures in here because it's raining outside."

The priest immediately went up to the videographer, thinking he was somehow responsible, grabbed him by the arm like he was an altar boy and once again snarled" What do you think you're doing?" He replied, "I'm just following the crowd!" The priest huffed and puffed for a few moments and said, "OK, I'll let you do it this time only, but you have to be out of here in twenty minutes." At that point, everyone knew they were in a hostile environment and they had already survived a baptism of fire. A twenty minute photo session followed and everyone was glad to escape the company of Father Cantankerous!

. . . . .

My Advice: The maid of honor, trying to be helpful, innocently led the lambs to the slaughter. Another service was planned after this one and time was of the essence. What the maid of honor didn't realize is these types of situations should be discussed by the bride and groom during the final consultation with the priest. Normally, the use of the church should be pre-arranged. Sometimes the photographer discusses this with the priest before the ceremony if time permits. An alternate plan is always essential when inclement weather is possible. Other indoor locations, classic buildings, banks or historical locations can quite often work very nicely. Be sure to have a backup plan!

THE BEARER OF ILL WILL

For the sake of convenience, the bride and groom made arrangements at a church near the restaurant where their reception would be held. They liked the physical beauty of the church and had met with the priest once or twice. During the meetings, he screened them for compatibility and to determine if they were getting married for the right reasons. The wedding day arrived and guests started filling the church. When I approached the priest to ask his policy on photos to be taken during the ceremony he angrily snapped, "You stay in that pew for the entire ceremony. Take all your photos from there!" He completely projected unwarranted hostility. Then, to make matters worse, during the actual ceremony he went into a first person tirade about when he was a boy growing up in his native country. This wasn't a Sunday morning sermon and had nothing to do with the wedding.

. . . . .

My Advice: When meeting with the person who'll be officiating your wedding, you must discreetly evaluate them while they're screening you. This process works both ways. You might not be compatible with the officiator. This individual certainly didn't have a friendly demeanor. The wedding sermon certainly wasn't planned. Inappropriate speeches never work. If you don't really know the officiator, you or your guests may fall victim to an unreasonable individual. Know your minister. Ask what the wedding sermon will be about and if you have any opportunity for input. Also ask about church policies pertaining to photography, videography, music, readers, etc. You don't want any unpleasant surprises on your wedding day.

THE LOUD MOUTH

It was a gazebo wedding in a beautiful outdoor setting. Two groups of chairs were arranged to form a middle aisle. The wedding party processed up the aisle to the gazebo and the ceremony was underway. A few minutes into the ceremony, someone's cell phone rang. To make matters worse, the individual answered the call, proceeded to talk loudly and disturbed the ceremony.

. . . . .

My Advice: What was this inconsiderate person thinking? No one wanted to hear this rude person's conversation, especially during a wedding ceremony. He could have left with his phone or merely shut it off. Did he think it was all right because he was outdoors? It's never acceptable to do this! That's why it's so important for the person officiating to make the announcement, "Please turn off all cell phones!" before the wedding procession even begins.

THE CHURCH IS CLOSED

The wedding ceremony ended and the wedding party and guests left the church to participate in a dove release and a receiving line in front of the building. Everyone had just left the church when the doors were locked. It meant that all the guests who were still on the church grounds were unable to access the restrooms. The videographer still had equipment to retrieve inside and this inconsiderate act created quite a bit of anxiety. Many times I have witnessed people, especially the elderly, looking for restrooms after a wedding ceremony.

. . . . .

My Advice: Someone must have been in a big hurry that day. Was it the clergy, the sexton or the custodian? Whoever made the decision to lock the doors so quickly certainly did everyone a disservice. Make sure you discuss, prior to your wedding day, how long the church will remain open after the ceremony. Are there restrooms available on the church grounds? Some older churches have restrooms in adjoining buildings. Guests should be forewarned that church doors will be locked at a particular time.

THE CRYING BABY

The church ceremony had just begun and the minister was beginning his prologue. Every time he started talking, a baby in the crowd started crying. This went on throughout the ceremony and not everyone thought it was cute. It was in fact, extremely disruptive. The baby was related to the bride so everyone tried to be tolerant.

. . . . .

My Advice: Sometimes the baby actually belongs to the bride and groom or a close relative. Nevertheless, a contingency plan

81

should be made so the child doesn't disrupt the entire ceremony. Most churches have soundproof crying rooms in the rear of the building. Hire a babysitter or delegate someone the baby is familiar with to take charge. If there's no crying room, the baby should be brought outside or at least in the rear of the church. Quite often, a bottle or some food will solve the problem.

THE DISHEVELED BRIDE

The church ceremony had just ended and the bride and groom formed a receiving line with their parents in front of the church. As the guests left the church they greeted each and every one while the guests congratulated the bride and groom. The bride's train was not bustled as yet and she quickly became tangled in her train while hugging and kissing her guests. Her veil was also pulled off accidentally while she was being hugged. Before long, the bride was a disheveled mess but the maid of honor, who was not in the receiving line, was nowhere to be found.

. . . . .

My Advice: This is a really common occurrence. It's the maid of honor's responsibility to tend to the brides needs on her wedding day. When the maid of honor is not in the receiving line, she must stay nearby, to help the bride out in her time of need. She should be equipped with a cold drink, tissues, lipstick, mints or anything else the bride might need. Of course, fixing the bride's train and her veil as needed would be one of her most important duties.

THE FIELD WEDDING

The wedding was taking place in a country setting that had a gazebo about one hundred yards from the main restaurant. Chairs were lined up in front of the gazebo, creating a center aisle. The grass surrounding this area could best be described as field grass. Unlike a putting green on a golf course, it was very lumpy. A white runner was unrolled and the wedding party started the processional. Moments after the runner was rolled out, it started to deteriorate. Before the first bridesmaid even stepped foot on the white runner, the wind had blown and twisted it into a roll. The wind continued to blow the carpet back and forth. This created quite a dilemma as the flimsy carpet became a real hazard. There was no time to stop the procession to remove it. Everyone coming down the aisle had to carefully zig zag to sidestep the runner. By the time the bride came down the aisle, she was happy just to bypass the runner and make it to the gazebo without tripping.

. . . . .

My Advice: The florist would love to sell you a white aisle runner, regardless of how impractical it might be. Flimsy aisle runners are never a good choice for outdoor weddings. If the lumpy ground doesn't make it look terrible, the wind will. On one occasion, the runner was weighed down with rocks. This made it look like a Stone Age wedding. However, I have seen the exception. For example, one time a groom stretched and staked the runner like a drum skin over the rough ground. This seemed to do the trick. Generally speaking, runners don't work outside. Perhaps an actual carpet would have been a better solution.

THE FLIGHT OF THE BUTTERFLIES

It was on outdoor ceremony on a warm day. As the guests arrived, they were handed a little box that contained a butterfly. The plan was, as soon as the newlyweds started down the aisle for their recessional, everyone would open their little boxes and a swarm of beautiful butterflies would grace the wedding. The newlyweds were announced and started down the aisle. The little boxes were opened but very few butterflies made it to the sky. Most made an attempt to fly, then fell to the ground. What should have been a delightful moment became one of great disappointment.

. . . . .

My Advice: Butterflies are placed into a dormant stage by chilling them. Perhaps they weren't shipped or stored properly or didn't have enough recovery time. Whatever the case might be, what would have been a fantastic photo opportunity turned into a disaster for the butterflies. It was a waste of time and money. When planning these types of things, be sure to inquire about the success rate and proper handling.

A HAZARDOUS SITUATION

The church ceremony ended and the newlyweds recessed out of the main entrance. Outside were two wicker cages filled with white doves. The bride and groom planned a dove release as soon as all the guests were outside. This tradition is perceived as a sign of good luck, romance and many years of happiness. The newlyweds each held a bird in their hands which they would release on the count of three. At the same time, the bird owners would open the doors to the two wicker cages and the flock of birds would fly away in unison. All the guests were outside and the bird people counted to three. The newlyweds tossed the birds up in the air and all the caged birds followed. The crowd cheered in delight. Just about everyone was thrilled by the result except the bride. Her hands were covered with bird droppings.

. . . . .

My Advice: This tradition, which can be fun, is not without risks. The birds can fly in someone's face and block it in the photographs or poop just about anywhere, including the bride's veil. The best solution is if the bride and groom stand about three or four feet apart, facing each other when releasing the birds. Wearing disposable gloves is not a bad idea either.

THE GARDEN WEDDING

It was the hottest day of the summer and a wedding ceremony was underway in a large garden behind a very large house. Two groups of chairs formed a makeshift aisle in the center. Behind each group of chairs was a large tub filled with ice and small bottles of water. The entire wedding party and all the guests were sitting in the torrid sun. The air was boiling and the humidity was unbearable. The ceremony started to drag on. The water ran out _very quickly. The guests started to wilt! Over one hundred people attended the ceremony. Only about half of them were fortunate enough to get water. Someone underestimated the situation and everyone was paying the price. Many guests had to leave before the ceremony was over in order to find respite in the reception tent, which was at least fifty yards away._

. . . . .

My Advice: Poor planning will always lead to problems. The weatherman can give some pretty good clues, but if no one is listening, what's the point? This type of situation was the result of an inexperienced wedding planner. Make sure that you have more cold drinks than you think you'll possibly need. You can drink any leftovers throughout the year or pass them on to friends.

THE MEDIEVAL WEDDING

The bride and groom were so enchanted with medieval times that they planned their wedding around that theme. All the guests were asked to wear medieval attire. A rustic country facility was reserved for the wedding. The big day arrived and all the costumed guests sat in their chairs, waiting for the bride to make her appearance. The plan was for her to arrive riding side saddle on a horse adorned with ribbon and lace. The horse trailer arrived and the horse was decorated accordingly. When the bride tried to mount the horse, the horse acted very nervously and wouldn't settle down. Everyone was concerned *about the bride's safety and so the big entrance on a horse was scratched.*

. . . . .

My Advice: It seems the wind blowing on the ribbons created a rustling noise that spooked the horse. As soon as the decorations were removed, the horse settled right down. The owner of the horse declared that because she was a young horse, she was fidgety. Perhaps an older horse would have worked out better. It seems that a dress rehearsal would have been in order for the horse. This is not always feasible when an unpredictable animal is being rented. Perhaps a more mature, docile horse should have been used. When adding unusual elements to your wedding, always expect the unexpected. In this case the only alternative was for the bride to walk down the aisle in the traditional way.

THE PHYSICAL OBSTRUCTION

The church ceremony began, and the wedding party proceeded down the aisle. The bride's largest relative, a six foot, six inch, 260 pound man, immediately positioned himself in the center aisle. Bending on one knee, he proceeded to photograph everyone walking down the aisle. With his large limbs sticking out he created a large obstacle that everyone had to walk around. This also created problems for me and the videographer. We were discreetly positioned near the front of the church. Picture the bride and her dad walking down the center aisle with a large unnecessary obstruction positioned halfway down the aisle. Not a pretty picture.

. . . . .

My Advice: Most brides and grooms would know who in their family would do this kind of thing. Ask them in advance to keep the center aisle clear. It would also be a good idea to ask the person officiating to make a brief announcement to that effect. A last minute solution would be to use hand signals with the thumb, while quietly verbalizing "move out of the way".

THE SCREECHER

It was a hot August day and the outdoor ceremony was taking place in a gazebo. It was the second marriage for both the bride and groom. They each had adult children who would be attending the wedding. The groom's daughter had volunteered to sing right after the vows and ring exchange. The DJ played the background music and she sang a popular love song. Trying out for a singing competition is one thing, but this young woman wouldn't have made it past the first round. She just couldn't sing on key no matter how hard she tried. The volume was cranked up and all the guests were wincing in pain due to the violent assault on their ears. My analysis is based on many comments I heard from other wedding guests. When the song was over, most of the guests sighed with relief.

. . . . .

My Advice: It was nice that the groom's daughter offered to sing but let's take a reality check. If she had no singing ability whatsoever, why not hire a professional or have a recording pumped through the DJ's sound system. Why torment the guests? Perhaps the groom was being kind to his daughter. He should have gracefully declined the offer and put everyone's ears to rest. A wedding ceremony should be a beautiful celebration and not an exercise in audible tolerance.

THE SPITEFUL SPOUSE

It was the second wedding for the groom. The groom and his first wife had already gone before a judge and resolved the divorce agreement. The plan was to finalize all the divorce paperwork one day before the groom's second wedding. This would allow the groom to get a marriage license as well. The judge had ordered the first wife to sign the divorce agreement. However, the temptation was too great and she absolutely refused to sign the divorce papers. She did this knowing she would throw a monkey wrench into the groom's plans to get married the next day. According to the groom she was jailed for contempt of court. The wedding day came and everyone went through the motions of a regular wedding. That is, except for the minister who couldn't legally marry them without a license. So they walked down the aisle, were blessed by the minister, exchanged rings, but they were not legally married. They went to their wedding reception and left for their honeymoon. It wasn't until after the groom's first wife spoiled his wedding day, did she agree to sign the divorce papers.

The couple eventually had a small civil ceremony to legalize their marriage.

. . . . .

My Advice: There's a good lesson to be learned here. Don't plan a second marriage until the first one is legally dissolved. The first wife truly enjoyed her role as the spoiler.

THE TOO LONG RECEIVING LINE

The wedding ceremony ended and a receiving line was set up outside in front of the church. The lineup included the parents and the entire wedding party. This totaled about 24 people. About two hundred guests exited the church and went through the receiving line. This took quite a bit of time and created an awkward situation, as many of the guests only knew either the bride, groom or their parents. So when they had to shake hands or kiss someone in the receiving line, it was usually someone that they didn't know.

. . . . .

My Advice: This is a common mistake. What they really needed here was an abbreviated receiving line that would include just the principals. The smaller group should consist of the newlyweds, their parents and maybe the best man and maid of honor. This would have expedited the whole process and eliminated most of the awkwardness that occurred. It would also have saved a lot of time. As previously mentioned, time is of the essence on a typical wedding day.

THE TRIPLE PLAY

Three weddings were scheduled at the same church on the same day. One wedding was scheduled for 9 AM, one at 10 and one at 11. The first wedding ran a few minutes late, ending just after 10 AM. But when all the people arrived for the second wedding, there was no parking outside because the first wedding was just finishing up. This turned the entire neighborhood into a virtual parking lot. When they did manage to find parking spaces, they were blocks away and had to walk to the church. In addition, there were no seats inside the church because the first wedding was still taking place. This made the second wedding late to start and later to finish. The chaos increased when the third limo arrived for the 11 AM wedding. The entire area became inundated with cars unable to move freely. This turned into a real nightmare.

. . . . .

My Advice: What was the church planner thinking? This never would have worked out. This was a situation destined for failure from the start. Whoever planned these weddings was naïve in thinking they would fit into such a restricted time frame. It's always a good idea to find out if anything else is happening at the church close to your wedding time. That way, you can anticipate any problems and plan accordingly.

THE VISUAL OBSTRUCTION

The wedding ceremony was taking place at an exclusive function facility noted for their elaborate outdoor gardens. The actual ceremony would be in a gazebo, situated in the middle of the floral landscape. The chairs were organized to form a center aisle which would accommodate the wedding processional and recessional. The wedding ceremony began and the entire wedding party proceeded down the aisle. The bride and her dad were no sooner at the gazebo, when the videographer jumped out and placed her camera and tripod in the center aisle adjacent to the front row seats. This created a visual obstruction in front of most of the guests throughout the entire ceremony. It also created a big problem for anyone with a camera, including me, the wedding photographer. The location of the videographer prevented any overview photos of the ceremony or the crowd without including the backside of the videographer.

. . . . .

My Advice: This "Me first and too bad for you" mentality doesn't work at a wedding. Granted, the strategic location of the videographer would certainly provide a good vantage point of the ceremony; however, they were totally impervious to the fact that their location would create problems for me and the wedding guests. Every wedding-related professional should be considerate of the next person and allow them to create the best possible product. To block the view of the ceremony is inexcusable. A simple solution would be to move the video camera and tripod in front of a seat, on one side of the aisle of the other. This way, the center aisle would remain clear. During your initial consultation, ask your videographers where they will be during your ceremony. Also ask them, "How many cameras will be used and will they use a remote microphone?" The use of a remote microphone means the cameras won't have to be in close proximity to record good sound.

THE WEDDING BY THE OCEAN

It was a late summer wedding located ocean side on some low lying cliffs. It was chosen for its spectacular view. The ceremony was just about to begin when fog started rolling in. The damp, cool mist obscured the picturesque view. When someone suggested a different location further inland, they were quickly overruled by the justice of the peace who said, "Don't mention that to the bride. Let's get this thing over with!"

. . . . .

My Advice: The justice of the peace was obviously trying to marry the couple as quickly as possible. He didn't care that the main reason they chose the place, the picturesque view, no longer existed. Had the wedding party moved further inland, the conditions would have been more favorable. Always discuss an alternate plan, especially when you're working outside in uncontrollable weather conditions.

TRAPPED IN THE LOT

The ceremony ended and the wedding party and parents recessed from the church. The plan was for the newlyweds to enter the limo and leave before the guests came out. They didn't want an impromptu receiving line outside of the church and time was limited. They also wanted a photo session in a scenic nearby location. Much to their dismay, the limo was boxed in. The church parking lot was very small, and some late arriving guests had parked in the only available space. The videographer and I were also boxed in.

. . . . .

My Advice: Waiting for all the parking lot blockers to move their cars turned into a big waste of time. All the key people should have parked near the street while the limousine drivers kept the exits clear. Use your time efficiently and anticipate potential problems.

TWO JUSTICES OF THE PEACE

The bride had scheduled an outdoor ceremony in a state park. About a half hour before the ceremony, two justices of the peace arrived and both claimed to have been retained for the wedding ceremony. This was a major glitch. Who was correct? They discussed it for a few minutes and arrived at a very diplomatic solution. They would both perform the ceremony simultaneously, acting as each other's assistant. They would split the fee and learn from the experience.

. . . . .

My Advice: Quite often the justice of the peace, hired to perform a civil ceremony, will not require any money up front. They usually get paid on the day of the event. In this case, the bride had contacted one JP and her mom another. Only one of them had returned the initial phone call and the other had not. How unprofessional and lackadaisical can you get? Fortunately, the real justice of the peace was gracious enough to bring the other on board. This is why you should reconfirm all your contacts at least one week prior to your wedding day.

TWO RECEIVING LINES

The church ceremony had just ended. The bride and groom just left the church and were hanging around outside. As the guests were leaving, they stopped to congratulate the bride and groom. This quickly turned into a spontaneous receiving line. This was not an unusual occurrence. People were strictly acting on their emotions and expressing their feelings. About an hour later, the wedding party was announced into the function hall. The function manager quickly set up a receiving line in the hall according to the original plan. No one stopped him or informed him that a spontaneous receiving line had formed outside of the church. A second receiving line was underway, which was a big waste of time. The majority of the people in attendance had already expressed their congratulatory remarks one hour earlier. It made for a very awkward redundant situation.

. . . . .

My Advice: Don't fall into this trap. There's a time to say something and a time to remain silent. This was definitely a time to speak up. Someone should have notified the banquet manager that there was a change in plans. Any time newlyweds hang around outside the church, people will naturally congratulate them. If you don't want this to happen, hide somewhere such as a spare room in the church or in the limo. One receiving line is usually sufficient. Many couples elect to forego the receiving line altogether. Instead they go around to each and every table to personally greet their guests and make them feel welcome. You will be in great demand that day. Use your time efficiently!

WHERE ARE THE RINGS?

Everyone was already at church when the groom and the best man arrived fifteen minutes late. They rushed into the church and met with the minister who immediately asked, "Where are the rings? Oh, I left them in the car. I can go get them," was the reply from the best man. "There's no time." the minister replied. "We have to start the ceremony!" So the wedding ceremony proceeded and the groom pretended to put an invisible ring on the bride's finger. Needless to say, the bride was shocked when no ring was presented.

. . . . .

My Advice: Running late never helps a situation. Getting the ring out of the car would have taken two minutes or less. For this particular minister, the additional delay would have been inexcusable. Things do happen, such as traffic jams, cutting yourself shaving, etc. Despite all this, do allow extra time to get ready and arrived relaxed and prepared.

You Stay in the Foyer

I had just arrived at the church. Before I could even open my mouth to talk to the officiator, the minister said, "You stay out in the foyer! I don't want you taking any photos during the ceremony, just during the processional and the recessional from the foyer!" No formal announcement was made to the guests regarding this no photo policy. During the actual wedding ceremony all the guests and relatives took pictures at will. Nothing was ever said to curtail this activity. I was the only one limited in the performance of my job.

. . . . . .

My Advice: Every church has their own policy on photography and videography during the wedding ceremony. Sometimes it's a church policy, and sometimes it's an arbitrary decision by the person in charge. By all means, these rules must be followed. When meeting with your officiator prior to the wedding day, be sure to discuss photo policies and optional solutions. In this particular case, I was the only one who had limits, which was an unpleasant surprise. Consequently, the bride and groom had to solicit ceremony photos from their guests. In this era of digital photography, excellent exposures can be made very discreetly. Without using a flash, cameras can now function very quietly. A balcony position with a zoom lens would render the photographer virtually undetectable. When this is done, it helps if the bride and groom are at least in profile. This allows for seeing the ring exchange even at great distances. In other words, if you're aware of the photographer's location, you would help the documentation by positioning your bodies accordingly.

THE DEADBEAT JUSTICE OF THE PEACE VS. THE SHOWMAN

The bride and groom hired a local justice of the peace to go on location and marry them in a gazebo surrounded by beautiful gardens. As the ceremony progressed, it was obvious that the J. P. was out to break the world's record for the fastest wedding ceremony. At least it seemed that way to me.

He barely greeted the guests. He read the introduction and proceeded with the vows and ring ceremony like a middle school student reading a homework assignment in front of the class. If he had a personality, he certainly didn't show it. I never once saw him smile. Upon completion of the ceremony he left quickly as though he had somewhere more important to go.

. . . . .

My Advice: You must know who you are hiring. Just because someone may be on a referral list doesn't mean they are necessarily the right person for you. Always ask for references and about other upcoming weddings he or she will be doing so you may observe them. This was an extreme example of someone discharging an obligation without putting any effort or feeling into their performance. The minimum effort put forth without any warmth left me with a flat feeling that something was missing.

Of course, I've also seen the other extreme where the minister or justice of the peace turned the ceremony into a Las Vegas show by wearing overly colorful outfits and acting more like he was doing a stand up comedy routine. By constantly calling attention to himself, it seemed he was more concerned with his own public image and showmanship. He undermined the importance of the bride and groom. They took a back seat to his comedy routine. You need to find a happy medium between the deadbeat and a showman.

CHAPTER 5

FORMAL PHOTO SESSION

A COUNTRY SMELL

The bride and her parents arrived in a horse drawn buggy. She was right on time for the ceremony. The plan was to take wedding party photos near the horse and buggy right after the ceremony. Once the ceremony was over, the wedding party gathered around the horse and buggy. Photos were taken post haste and the group started to disband. Within seconds, the horse started to urinate on the hot asphalt. The stream of urine was so forceful that the bride barely escaped the splashing. The odor was quite foul. Had she not left when she did, her gown would have smelled so badly that she would have had to change into something else.

. . . . .

My Advice: When working with an unpredictable animal such as a horse, the bride should be extremely cautious. She should take great care in avoiding the tail end of the horse, where a mishap can occur. Of course, everything is relative. If the bride grew up in horse country she'd probably dismiss this as a big joke. Ask yourself, "Do you really want to know what horse pee smells like?"

A TRIP TO THE CAROUSEL

The newlyweds wanted wedding party photos taken at a local carousel. As soon as the wedding ceremony was over, the entire wedding party was shuttled via limousine to a nearby historic carousel. They had arranged to have it totally to themselves for one hour. The parents and grandparents went along as well. The plan was to photograph all the parent groups first and then turn the wedding party loose on the carousel. What they didn't anticipate was the elderly grandparents had difficulty negotiating the moving step up to the carousel. Even when it was stopped, it was still a little wobbly. This delayed things a little bit. They literally had to be lifted up. Once the parents and grandparents were free to go, I concentrated on the wedding party. The party included a few young children. They had to be placed on stationary horses because they had to have a parent standing nearby. Another hindrance was a safety railing that surrounded the carousel and partially obstructed a clear view of the wedding party.

. . . . .

My Advice: The physical layout of a typical carousel doesn't easily lend itself to very large groups. The many vertical poles and busy backgrounds definitely competes with the subject matter. The visual obstructions require a little more time to organize a large group. These sessions usually cannot be done quickly unless you hurry the poses and are not too fussy about the backgrounds. In this case, the parents and grandparents should have been photographed elsewhere.

BEE CAREFUL, OR CANCAN IN THE CLOVER

The bride lived in a modern home in the country. Directly behind her home was a large field covered in clover. Adjoining this field were gently sloping hills adorned with a plush natural woodland. This is why she wanted all her formal wedding party photos taken in this area. She simply loved her surroundings.

Once the church ceremony ended, the entire wedding party and their families returned to the bride's home. All the bridesmaids wore long dresses with hoop skirts. Several layers of netting served to fill out the bottom of their dresses which was the style at the time.

As soon as all the bridesmaids gathered around the bride for a group photo, one of them suddenly ran away. She lifted her dress up, flailing her hemline in the air while yelling and screaming hysterically. Her unusual manner was reminiscent of an out of control cancan dancer. Not knowing if the bridesmaid was trying to be funny, everyone laughed and looked on in disbelief. As her behavior continued, someone finally shouted "What's wrong with you?" She blurted out, "Something flew up my dress and stung me a few times!" You can imagine her fear with one or more stinging insects trapped inside her skirt. All of a sudden the mood became very somber and the rest of the bridesmaids quickly ran out of the field. The injured bridesmaid was brought into the house where she received first aid. All the groomsmen offered to assist with first aid but she refused.

. . . . .

My Advice: All the petticoat layers filling out the bridesmaids skirts acted as a large net, trapping some stinging insects (most likely, bees). Of course this could have happened with any style dress. However, the full hoop bottom only increased the chance of this happening.

Granted, this is a highly unusual situation, but a few precautions could have been taken to minimize the likelihood of this type of incident. First, someone could have cut and bagged the clover, reducing it to a very short level. Second, the bridal party should have avoided lingering in any field of clover or flowers where bees are known to be active. Of course, the threat was not perceived until it was too late. Finally, the judicious use of perfume might be an appropriate idea when the bridal party is to be photographed in an outdoor, wooded area. The more fragrant you are, the more likely you are to attract a variety of insects. I have personally witnessed many a perfume ritual when bridesmaids were getting ready for a wedding. The practice of spraying perfume all over one's legs and body might be best done at the reception.

BLINDED BY THE LIGHT

The bride had a very large family and wedding party. So she requested that I take some structured family photos at a designated time. This was not an unusual request, as large families rarely get together at the same time. This will never take the place of actual wedding candids, but it will commemorate the family tree and how everyone looked on that day. The people were assembled and the photo session began. Two minutes into the session, the videographer set his equipment right next to me, turned on his bright light and started doing freeze frames. The bright light he was using caused everyone to squint horribly. This created terrible expressions and he was quickly asked to stop.

· · · · ·

My Advice: The videographer is hired to record action and sound. He shouldn't be trying to duplicate the still photographer's effort by shooting over his shoulder. Granted, modern digital video cameras can shoot under very low lighting conditions. This usually precludes shining bright lights directly into people's eyes. However, they should be able to think for themselves and seek out all the surrounding activity that occurs when a large group of people get together. There's always a lot of spontaneous interaction which can best be captured most effectively with the sights and sounds of video. When consulting a videographer prior to your wedding day, ask them if they create videos from their own perspectives or copy the still photographer's images. Look at samples of their work and see if they're capturing any emotions, hugs, tears or surprised expressions.

DUCK-DOO IS GREEN GOO

The bride selected a scenic historical park with an old fashioned windmill and a lovely little pond for some wedding party photos. The stream which fed the pond and the pond itself, was frequented by numerous ducks and geese. As to be expected, the ground surrounding this area was heavily inundated with fowl droppings. The bride was ever so careful where she walked. However she did succeed in getting some green stains along the hemline of her dress.

. . . . .

My Advice: Whenever ducks and geese congregate in an area for any period of time, they will litter the ground. Bird droppings make terrible stains on a wedding gown. I can't tell you how many times I've seen this happen. Be aware of the hazards and deal with them accordingly. When you stop for a photo session, why not send out a few people to scout the area looking for possible threats. This is a good assignment for someone not wearing high heels or a dress. You can always bring a small shovel and pail filled with sand. This will allow you to cover or remove any animal droppings in the area.

FORMALS AT THE WINERY

After the church ceremony, the bride and groom had planned to have some formal wedding photos taken at a nearby winery. The vineyard was located about twenty miles away on the banks of a very picturesque river. The crest of the hill was lined with rows of mature oak trees. The hillside going down to the river was dotted with neatly arranged grape vines going all the way down to the river. This location would certainly enhance any group photos taken there. The bride and groom had made the necessary arrangements with the owners several weeks prior to the wedding date. The big day arrived and the wedding limousine drove down the dirt road that led to the vineyard. Everyone was immediately shocked when they saw a very large white tent of circus proportions erected in the middle of the oak trees. The grounds were also bristling with people. Apparently, the vineyard was having a wine tasting event that day and neglected to tell the newlyweds. This made wedding photos extremely challenging and the wedding party was relegated to a less attractive location.

. . . . .

My Advice: The bride and groom neglected to ask one very important question: Was anything else going on there that day or nearby that might impact their use of the grounds? The ride to the vineyard took half an hour. Time was of the essence. They couldn't go elsewhere so they had to make the best of a bad situation. What should have been an ideal situation turned into a struggle to omit the background activity. Make sure you take the time to ask all the relevant questions when going on location.

FROSTY TOES

It was a winter wedding and the indoor church ceremony had just concluded. Outside a few inches of snow adorned the trees and ground. The bride had selected an outdoor location to have some artistic photos taken of her and her new husband. The area she selected was certainly picturesque. The location included several large pine trees atop of a knoll that were all covered with snow. The bride wore a white mid-length fur coat over her gown with open toe shoes. The groom wore a traditional black tuxedo, a black top coat and typical black dress shoes. The photo session began as planned. The bride and groom were both standing in ankle deep snow. I worked as fast as humanely possible to accommodate their requests. That's what I was getting paid for, to take the photos they wanted, not to second guess their wishes.

Fifteen minutes into the session, the bride had had enough. Her feet were freezing and she was miserably cold. The session ended rapidly and she went inside a warm building. The maid of honor quickly removed the bride's shoes to reveal her beet red feet. She then wrapped the bride's feet in some warm dry towels to ease her discomfort.

. . . . .

My Advice: Outside photos in the snow is a fun idea. The bride's fur coat was very practical but her shoes were not. It doesn't take a genius to figure this one out. She didn't plan accordingly. She took care of her upper body warmth but the open toe shoes were a big mistake. She should have brought some warm white boots. The typical wedding gown usually will hide your feet, especially when you're sinking into the snow.

HORSE SCENTS

The bride arrived at the church with her parents in a horse and buggy. Directly across the street was an elaborate building with a fancy drive through portico. It was a hot summer day and the portico would provide shade for the horse and buggy while the wedding ceremony was taking place. The bride very much wanted to document her fancy ribbon decorated coach. The plan was immediately after the ceremony the entire wedding party, about twenty people, would cross the street for a formal photo session. The portico provided open shade, which eliminated harsh shadows.

This was an ideal photo location. Before the ceremony was over, the horse urinated in the parking lot. The carriage was parked right under the portico where the photos were scheduled to be taken. The ceremony ended, and this mishap was discussed with the bride. She basically said, "Full speed ahead, let's go on with our plans!" So the wedding party was posed in and around the carriage. The people standing in the urine were less than thrilled.

. . . . .

My Advice: The bride was very brave and daring to do this. Of course, the newlyweds were sitting in the open carriage, so they weren't greatly impacted by the aroma. The area surrounding the portico was a parking lot. Given the situation, she really didn't have much of a choice. I'm sure there was an outdoor water faucet in the immediate area. A little forethought would have had a hose hooked up to wash things down. The horse and buggy should have been parked elsewhere until it was time for photos. Fortunately, this happened during the digital age, so the large wet area under the carriage was retouched.

LOSING THE LIGHT

An evening wedding took place outdoors in a beautiful garden area. The bride and groom specifically asked for outside photographs. When the ceremony was finished, the guests were invited indoors to partake in a cocktail hour. The wedding party remained outside with their families to be photographed on the spectacular grounds.

The formal photo session began and everything was working out as planned. That is, until the wait staff brought out several tables with drinks and hors d'oeuvres. Everyone immediately stopped what they were doing and flocked to the refreshments.

. . . . .

My Advice: This was clearly a conflict of interest. The bride and groom wanted outside photos but when the sun set, the sky went dark and the photos were much less attractive. This situation happens all the time. You can't blame the wedding party for being hungry and thirsty. Wedding days can be very lengthy and tiring. The solution is a compromise. Groups should eat in shifts. Anyone not required to be in a group photo should partake in the refreshments. This should be worked out in detail with the caterer before the wedding day. Any competent photographer should know what time the sun sets and how long it should take to complete the formal shots. What he won't know is how long the ceremony will last and how much cooperation he will receive.

SAND ANGELS

The bride and groom had a late spring wedding. It was a gorgeous sunny day. She had requested a photo session at a nearby scenic beach. This beach not only had a great water view, but rolling dunes of silky smooth sand. The wedding party consisted of eighteen adults and two children. The flower girl was about six years old and the ring bearer still in diapers, was barely three. As soon as the boy's parents took their eyes off him for a minute, he was laying on his back doing a sand angel. Someone must have shown him how to do a snow angel the previous winter.

Try to imagine a three year old wearing a tuxedo while flailing his arms and legs in the sand. It was cute and humorous but he turned into a sandy disaster in no time at all. He quickly had sand in his eyes, hair and in every place where sand will go. He really needed a bath. After the photo shoot, the ring bearer's parents had to literally strip him down in the limousine and overhaul him on the way to the reception.

. . . . .

My Advice: Put a child in a candy store, and they're going to want candy. Put a child in a sand box, and they're going to play in the sand. Supervision is exactly that, using your super vision to keep someone out of trouble. When young children are involved, it's sometimes prudent to hire a babysitter. The photo shoot was a big success but a big burden was placed on the parents of the ring bearer.

THE AD LIB PHOTO LIST

The ceremony was over and it was time for the formal photo session. However, no written list had been given to me before the wedding. A structured plan was missing. Both the bride and groom wanted to take family and wedding party photos but people were missing from both groups. Finding these people took quite a bit of time. As a result of this, the photo session had to be cut short.

. . . . .

My Advice: Creating a predetermined list of photo requests prior to your wedding day is essential. This creates a blueprint for what the sequence of events will be. The list should be formulated according to the chronological events of the day plus any special photos. For example, if your grandmother is elderly and will only attend the church ceremony, then she will have to be photographed before or after the ceremony. All the people that will be in the formal groups should be notified in advance of where you expect them to be and at what time. One side of the family, either the bride's or the groom's should be the focus at one time.

Groups containing very old people or very young children should be done first. People who can't walk or stand very well should be provided with a seat.

If it's a public location, you must do research to determine that no competing events such as parades, road construction, etc., are taking place in or on the way to that area. Make sure the photographer gets a copy of the list well in advance. Finally, delegate someone on each side of the family to help find people. Once found, have them stand nearby so they will be available when needed.

Note: The "My Advice" to the following story called "The Conflicting Request Lists" also pertains to similar problems. Essentially this story was about having no list at all. The next story is about conflicting photography lists.

THE CONFLICTING REQUEST LISTS

About three weeks before the wedding, the bride gave me a list of special photo requests that she'd like taken on her wedding day. A week before the wedding, the bride gave me a second request list. Many of the second requests contradicted the first request list. It was so confusing that I asked the bride to clarify the conflicting information and to please put her requests in the chronological sequence of the day. On the wedding day the bride gave me a third list. This time it was hand written and not in any particular order. Deciphering three conflicting request lists was highly confusing, especially when there was no real time on the wedding day to sit down and analyze the bride's cryptographic puzzle.

· · · · ·

My Advice: If you want to confuse the photographer, this is what you would do. The correct way to itemize your special photo requests is to determine what will happen first. A typical wedding day is like a five act play. It begins with the getting ready photos at wherever the bride is preparing for the wedding. The next sequence is the actual ceremony, then a formal photo session, followed by the reception (wedding banquet) and finally finishing with a going away sequence. This is the typical chronological sequence of events but it's certainly not written in stone.

The next important point is how you'll describe the people that will be in your photo requests. You can use proper nouns and write, "Uncle Jim and Aunt Alice Johnson with Lucy, Mark and James." Using everyone's complete proper name will only complicate things. You can also simplify the process while revealing clearer information. For example, the newlyweds with the bride's Aunt Alice, Uncle Jim and their three kids. As in the previous story, I would highly recommend that you delegate someone on each side of the family as a people finder. The photographer can't be smoothly progressing through these group photos and looking for people at the same time. Also, make sure the photographer receives your list at least one week before your wedding. This will allow for analysis and questions if any arise, and they usually do.

THE BIG CHILL

It was a Valentine's Day wedding at a beautiful waterfront restaurant. It was sunny and about thirty-two degrees. Some people may consider this a heat wave, depending on where you're from. The bride and groom thought so. They insisted that the entire wedding party be photographed on the beach right outside the restaurant. The bride and bridesmaids all were wearing off the shoulder dresses with furry shawls. They looked nice but weren't very warm. The wind was coming off the water at about twenty-five miles per hour. This created a wind chill well below freezing. Needless to say, the wedding party was freezing and miserable for the entire ten minute photo shoot. It took quite some time indoors for the wedding party to recover from this ordeal.

. . . . .

My Advice: To insist that the wedding party take photos outside under such extreme conditions might be pushing the limits of reasonable requests. They should have planned this event better. Renting fur coats might have been a good solution. Even something as simple as a couple of color coordinated quilts might have taken the chill out of the situation.

The Egg Heads

It was during the hottest days of August about two days before the groom was to be married. The groom and all the groomsmen decided to shave their heads for a real cool look. Despite the bride's protests, the men went ahead with their plans. On the wedding day, they all looked like they just finished military basic training. There was one big oversight on their part. They all worked outside in the construction industry so their faces and necks that weren't protected at work were deeply tanned. Their freshly shaved heads however, were as pale as a carton of white eggs. Now bald can be beautiful, but what these guys created was a two toned mess. They looked like aliens from outer space. Not only did they look ridiculous on the wedding day, but they looked really peculiar in all the photos in which they appeared.

. . . . .

My Advice: Their pale heads were definitely a distraction. It also generated an additional expense for the bridal couple, as it required extensive retouching for the finished photo album. In this era of spray tans, this situation could have been inexpensively remedied in less than two hours' time.

THE GROOM MELTDOWN

By the end of the wedding ceremony, the rain had stopped and the sun shined brightly. The bride very much wanted to have her photos taken at the beach and she was going to get her wish fulfilled. The sandy beach was about eighteen miles away, so the wedding party of about sixteen people climbed into the limousine. The groom grabbed his cooler loaded with alcoholic beverages and brought it with him in the limo. The wedding party started partying all the way to the beach. This was about a half hour ride. When they arrived at the beach, the groom was already partially drunk. At that point he didn't want to cooperate with the bride's requests, he just wanted to keep drinking. The groom's photos were finally taken under protest, but not before he had an unflattering, childish breakdown.

. . . . .

My Advice: Whenever the wedding party has had too much alcohol too soon, the cooperation factor diminishes. If the wedding party is a drinking crowd, restrict the use of alcohol until after they have performed their job of cooperating with the bride's requests for group photos. This scenario is the exception and not the rule. Drinking on an empty stomach can quickly turn into an intolerable situation. Why not bring finger food and soft drinks in the limousine? This would appease hunger and thirst and keep the group sober.

THE HISTORICAL SOCIETY

The newlyweds planned to have formal group photographs taken at the local historical society building. This seemed like a good idea as the weather was inclement. So, right after the wedding ceremony finished, the wedding party headed to the historical society. On arrival, much to their dismay, they found the building quite crowded with antiques. Heavy, musty curtains didn't add to the ambiance and blocked most of the daylight. Everyone made the best of a bad situation, then left as quickly as they could.

. . . . .

My Advice: When making arrangements to use or rent a given location, make sure you're familiar with the place. Don't just send them your deposit and assume that everything will be to your satisfaction. Go look at the place yourself! If you can't do this, have someone take a video to show you.

THE HOUSE OF MARBLE

The bride and groom scheduled their wedding for an historic mansion. This extravagant house was built during the Gilded Age during the late 1800's when all the wealthy industrialists were trying to impress each other with their opulent homes.

This particular building, like many other historic mansions, was eventually taken over and run by the local historical society. They would rent the location for different functions to generate the revenue needed to maintain the property. After their church wedding, the bride and groom arrived at this elegant facility. They wanted to take photos on the balcony overlooking the water, but they were shocked to find out that no one was allowed on the balcony for any reason. This and other stringent restrictions put a real hindrance on their photo plans.

. . . . .

My Advice: Quite often when a luxurious building is advertised, they'll describe it as having beautiful marble staircases, fireplaces and overlooking balconies. Whether you can actually use these features that are described is uncertain. You must ask a few pertinent questions when meeting with the booking manager. "Are there any restrictions? May I use the balconies? Who is allowed to go where? How close to the water can I go?" etc. You get the idea. Be ultra-inquisitive. Don't be so enthralled with the place that you don't find out what you actually can and cannot do!

THE LARGE BRIMMED HAT

Wedding fashions are very trendy. At this particular wedding, the fashion was for the bride to wear a very large hat. It was pulled down a little lower on one side of her face. Whenever the bride was in bright sun, a heavy dark shadow would be cast on one or both sides of her face. This made my job very difficult. The challenge was now to provide enough light under her hat by using an electronic flash to lighten the shadows.

. . . . .

My Advice: Isn't the objective to see the bride's face throughout the day? When this bride's head was tilted down, you couldn't see her face at all. I've included this story in case any future brides, mothers or grandmothers are considering wearing a large brimmed hat to a wedding. Consider the ramifications and plan accordingly.

The Photo Marathon

The wedding reception was scheduled for about five hours. Right after the main course was served, the bride, groom, wedding party, and the parents went outside for some formal group photos. This was not unusual as formal group shots had not been taken yet. What was unusual was that the photo session lasted two and a half hours. The bride was more concerned with being photographed in every corner of the scenic gardens than she was with visiting with her guests. It also compromised the time frame for other planned activities.

. . . . .

My Advice: This photo session was excessive because the guests were ignored. It's not the photographer who makes these decisions. He's paid to follow directions whether they are reasonable or not. What happened here was very inconsiderate. Some brides are just too preoccupied with the photography and not attentive enough to their wedding guests.

119

THE PUBLIC GARDEN

The bride and groom selected a very popular public garden in a big city to have wedding party and family photos taken. All the key people arrived in limos and disembarked. The videographer and I drove our own cars. There was no off street parking available in the immediate area. The limo drivers stayed in their cars while parked in the breakdown lane. Everyone else left their cars unattended in the same area. We had no choice. After the formal photo session was over, the drivers of the unattended cars all found $75 parking tickets on their windshields. The limo drivers didn't receive any.

· · · · ·

My Advice: This was another classic example of poor planning. When selecting an exclusive location especially in a big city where parking is notoriously tight don't forget about the hired help. Consider a shuttle bus or a designated parking area. Sometimes the photographer and videographer can leave their cars elsewhere and ride in the limo. This is only feasible when extenuating circumstances prevail. Be considerate! You must look at the total picture when planning your wedding.

THE SCENIC PHOTO LOCATION

The bride and groom had selected an old historic fort which was part of a state park for their wedding formals. This scenic location

*included rocky ledges, fast moving tidal water, large rock forma-
tions, windswept trees, old gun turrets and a grassy area. Included
in the very large wedding party were two fairly young flower girls
and two young ring bearers. The parents of these children were
also part of the wedding party. The plan was to photograph all the
groups that included the children first. This is usually a good idea,
as kids will become impatient really fast when they're restrained
in an area they perceive as fun. They behaved very well and in ten
minutes time were free to enjoy themselves. Their parents were still
occupied with group photos, so only the grandparents were free to
supervise the children. The kids were a bundle of energy. They ran
from one potential hazard to the next. The grandparents couldn't
keep up. It seems that every thirty seconds they were on the brink
of another potential disaster. This created a big distraction and a
great deal of anxiety. The group photos were quickly finished and
the hazardous situation was eliminated.*

My Advice: Scenic locations have a tendency to be precarious
as well. With plenty of places to fall, no one realized the hazards that this location posed until it was too late. Sometimes
it's feasible to hire a babysitter to tend to the young children
in circumstances such as these. What if the maid of honor was
the mother of one of these small children? How is she going to
tend to the bride's needs and take care of her youngsters at the
same time? Anticipate these situations and think about the consequences. Be sure you have someone on hand who can keep
up with the children when their parents are busy.

THE UNCOOPERATIVE GROOM

From the beginning, the bride let me know she really loved being in photos. However, she said the groom hated it. It takes two to marry and I couldn't just photograph the bride all day. The groom resisted any attempts to be photographed. That is until a cousin of his picked up her camera and put him through a series of "do this" and "do that" photo sequences. She stopped just short of having him stand on his head or swing from a chandelier.

. . . . .

My Advice: This was a pretty clear sign that there was a conflict of interest. The bride wanted one thing, the groom another. A request to do strictly candid photos all day would have been more practical. This is actually easier to do when your subject is being uncooperative. This totally photojournalistic approach can work out quite well unless you have a very large wedding party. Let's say you have fourteen or more people in your wedding party. Don't expect them to all look in the same direction and the same time without a little prodding. Granted, you can get bits and pieces of the group here and there, but if you want a flattering group shot, the groom's cooperation is essential. Be sure you let the photographer know exactly what you want and what you expect up front. Keep in mind that a certain amount of cooperation is required.

Too Hot to Trot

It was the dog days of August and the temperature was predicted to be close to 100°. The groom and all the groomsmen wore black tuxedos with vests. After the wedding ceremony was over, it was time for a formal photo session. The groom however, was feeling faint. He had to remove his jacket and sit in the shade and recover with a cold drink.

. . . . .

My Advice: What were they thinking? A black tuxedo in the sun is a solar collector. If you aren't hot enough with a vest and jacket, the sun will certainly finish you off. You probably don't think about that when you go to the tuxedo shop in the middle of January. Go online and look up the average temperature for your wedding day and plan accordingly. A lightweight summer suit would have been a more logical choice for the hottest days of summer. Having cold drinks readily available is also helpful. A cooler of frozen face cloths will help. Simply moisten them with water, put them in individual bags and freeze them before the wedding. A frozen face cloth when held on the neck or face will lower the body temperature for quite some time and can be quite refreshing.

Photos by the Fireplace

It was a night wedding at the beginning of winter. The reception was taking place in a large restaurant during the holiday season. Inside the facility was a large marble fireplace. The mantle was gaudily decorated to reflect the season. This was the location the _bride wanted her formal wedding photos taken. The fireplace was lit and the fire was roaring. After all, what's a fireplace for if it's not lit on a cold winter's night?_

The wedding party consisted of twenty-four people. The group was organized and the photo session ensued. Everything was flowing smoothly until some members of the wedding party had to move away from the fireplace. It was simply too hot to stay there for any length of time. There wasn't any other suitable location to photograph a group of this size so the photo session was temporarily postponed until the fire died down.

. . . . .

My Advice: This was a big time waster because the same group had to be organized later and they were already in a party mood. Photo requests in front of fireplaces are actually quite common. In fact, this location can work quite well if the mantle isn't overly decorated or the fireplace is blazing away, giving off oppressive heat. When mantles are too cluttered, the photo session becomes an exercise in not having background objects looking like they are protruding from someone's head.

Large wedding parties are best photographed on staircases when available. Going outside for photos on a cold winter night is usually not an option. Large groups require more time and space to photograph. Sitting the bridesmaids on chairs with the groomsmen standing behind them will effectively reduce the space needed to accomplish this feat.

Later, the bride expressed displeasure with all the distracting holiday decorations. _Brides, be realistic with your expectations!_ When booking a facility, always ask to see what the hall might look like during a particular time of year. Most banquet facilities have photo albums that would show you exactly what to expect during the different seasons.

A Flower among the Thorns

The bride wanted her formal wedding photos taken in a famous rose garden that was in close proximity to the reception hall. Upon arrival, the bride was cautioned by the caretaker not to get too close to the rose bushes. The photo session began and it wasn't too long before a slight breeze blew the bride's exceptionally long veil into the thorns. The bridesmaids rushed to her aid and carefully pulled out her veil from the thorny bushes but not without great difficulty. The end result was a veil full of small holes.

. . . . .

My Advice: Even though she was forewarned about the hazards her gown would face, she went ahead with her plans. Rose gardens don't provide a very lush background. In fact, the thorns greatly outnumber the flowers. Placing a bride near rose bushes is like putting her in a field of barb wire. Don't do it! It's a recipe for disaster. Instead, seek out a backdrop with lush, dense greenery without thorns. Ask your photographer to keep the background softly out of focus so it won't become a distraction.

CHAPTER 6

THE

RECEPTION

They Stooped and Rose to the Occasion

It was cake cutting time at the reception. The cake table was situated in a remote corner of the hall. The wait staff lifted the cake table and carried it to the center of the dance floor. This would enable all the guests to easily see the bride and groom cut the cake. As they put the table down, one of the legs broke off while everyone watched. The tilting table sent the cake to the floor. Everyone watching, including the bride and groom were totally horrified. Fortunately, the cake didn't fall frosting side down. The bottom two layers, though a little mangled, survived remarkable well. Once everyone recovered from the shock, the bride and groom stooped down and cut what remained of their cake. They then fed each other, which drew a long resounding cheer from the crowd.

. . . . .

My Advice: The cake table was barely more than a card table with flimsy legs. It didn't take much pressure on one leg for it to snap off. However, the bride and groom didn't roll over and play dead. They turned a negative into a positive, and carried the crowd with them. The remainder of the cake couldn't be served to the wedding guests. Cakes can easily cost several hundred dollars. This is why you must ask the restaurant or function hall if they're insured for such a mishap. The newly-weds shouldn't take the loss for this. The fault clearly lies with the restaurant.

A PARTIAL TOAST

The best man was handed the microphone to propose a toast to the newlyweds. He had written down exactly what he was going to say on a large index card that he held in one hand. He began with, "I'd like to propose a toast, etc." When he was finished, he sat down. However, no one raised their glasses because they were never prompted to do so.

. . . . .

My Advice: The guests need an audible command such as "Now let us all raise our glasses" or "Cheers." This indicates yes indeed, the toast is over and now is the time to salute the couple. With an audible cue in whichever language you choose, all the glasses are raised in unison.

A PERFECT STRIKE

The reception was underway and the main course of food was just consumed. The bride and her dad just went out onto the dance floor, and the father daughter dance had begun. The function manager had decided that they needed to move an eight foot banquet table that was adjacent to the dance floor to another location. This was quite a distraction to the emotional father/ daughter dance that was transpiring. When the manager and a waiter started to maneuver the table out of the way, they bumped into dad with the edge of the table, knocking him onto his behind. The guests were quite shocked and the father of the bride was furious.

. . . . .

My Advice: Was the table being moved to make more room on the dance floor? Moving tables is a common occurrence when space is limited and there's a lot of guests crowded into a small hall. Knocking dad over is a totally unforgivable act. He's the person who usually pays the bills. This was quite a conflict of interest. Was there a breakdown of communication between the disc jockey/band leader and the function manager? Whenever an activity is about to take place, the person running the show should communicate with the function manager. "Is this a good time for the father/ daughter dance? If not, when?"

AN ELECTRIFYING MOMENT

The bride hired a very popular musician. He had exceptional singing abilities and could play at least a half a dozen musical instruments. He would prepare all his background music ahead of time. On the wedding day he would play or sing the lead in sync with his pre-recorded background music. The combination of the two really emulated a full band sound. The bride had retained a very reputable restaurant noted for its fine dining and luxurious atmosphere. The entertainer arrived as scheduled and set up his state of the art electronic equipment. The wedding party was lined up outside the hall and introductions were about to begin.

The one man band powered up to perform the final equipment check when he received a powerful electric jolt through his microphone. This electrical surge simultaneously fried all his primary equipment. He immediately notified the function manager of the situation. The manager was very unsympathetic and replied, "Well, no one else has ever had that problem before, so it must be your equipment!" Realizing the mess that he was in, he immediately asked if he could run his backup equipment through the restaurant's public address system. No problem, the function manager gladly obliged. The entertainer started his introductions and did the best he could under this situation. Instead of a full stereo sound, he was limited to a monaural (single channel) sound.

The musician kept getting jolted throughout the evening while using the house microphone. This led him to believe that it wasn't his equipment after all. The next day he returned to the restaurant, bringing a master electrician with him to determine the source of the problem. After evaluating the power source, the electrician determined that the available outlets provided for him contained 115 volts and well as 220 volts. It seems that some electrical work had been done on the grounds outside the function room, and a live 220 line was hooked up to the ground wire.

. . . . .

My Advice: This was a rare occurrence but it could have happened to anyone. The musician now brings an electrical voltage tester with him to all his functions. Both the bride and musician were compensated by the restaurant for their mutual nightmare. It might be a good idea to ask the musician or DJ if they have a backup plan. A better idea would be to ask the function manager if any repairs or remodeling has been done recently in or around the function hall. If so, has anyone tested the electrical outlets?

The last logical question would be, "What if there's a power outage? Do you have adequate generators to keep the celebration up and running? "

AN UNFORTUNATE COLLISION

It was an afternoon wedding banquet. A large contingent of young children were running around the dance floor and its perimeter. A wedding guest had finished his wine and held his long stem glass low. He was on his way back to the bar for a refill when a youngster about three years of age ran right into the man's glass. The glass broke and the child received a large gash on his forehead. He was quickly brought to the hospital for stitches and the mess was cleaned up.

. . . . .

My Advice: Quite often groups of children are allowed to run freely at wedding banquets. This is definitely a recipe for disaster. More supervision was clearly needed here. A creative solution is to provide a group babysitter to entertain the kids. Giving them gift packs with an assortment of small toys and coloring books usually helps. Finally, designating a table or specific area in one corner of the reception hall just for the children is also a good idea.

BLACK TIE EVENT

The wedding reception was being held at an exclusive private country club. All the guests were notified in their wedding invitations that this would be a black tie event requiring formal attire for all men and women. The videographers were a husband and wife team. Both wore tuxedo shirts with black bow ties. He wore black tuxedo pants and had a black jacket to put on. She wore a black skort (shorts made to look like a skirt) with her outfit. The function manager noticed this upon her arrival and promptly notified her that her outfit was unacceptable. Unless she went home to change, there would be no food or beverage service provided for her. She lived a great distance from where the event was being held so going home to change was not a viable option. He also notified the entire wait staff of this situation and she was ostracized throughout the event.

. . . . .

My Advice: Was she capable of performing her job as well under these conditions? I think not. Her attire was more suitable for a casual event. Was it really her fault? Remember, if you're holding a black tie event, you must let everyone know, including the hired help. In this case, the videographers were never sent an invitation and didn't know this was a black tie event.

BOTCHED UP
INTRODUCTIONS

All the guests were seated and the DJ started introducing the wedding party into the room. It was a large wedding party with about two dozen people of various nationalities. Within the first five or six introductions it was clear the DJ couldn't pronounce many of the names properly. In fact the order of his introductions didn't even correspond with the way the wedding party and parents were lined up. It became a real comedy of errors. The guests breathed a collective sigh of relief when the bride and groom were finally introduced.

. . . . .

My Advice: This happens quite often. Give it the attention it deserves. It is imperative that the DJ, band leader, maître d', function manager or whoever will be making the introductions receives a complete list of everyone who will be introduced into the reception in the exact order they will be entering the room. The announcer should talk to everyone lined up outside the entrance and review the sequence of people as well as the proper pronunciation of their names. Problems usually occur when the wedding is running late and this step is rushed or completely eliminated.

Bubbles Galore

The guests were all lined up around the entrance to the banquet hall and the newlyweds were about to be announced. All the guests were given a small container of bubbles to celebrate the newlyweds' entrance. The bride and groom were announced and walked into the hall. All the guests were blowing as many bubbles as possible. The newlyweds went right into their first dance while the guests continued with their bubble making. A few minutes into the dance, the bride and groom started slipping. The soapy bubbles on a smooth floor created a hazardous situation.

. . . . .

My Advice: Leather soled shoes and soap on a smooth surface is a recipe for disaster; however it does provide a beautiful photo opportunity. Many function halls frown on the use of bubbles indoors on a hard surfaced floor. Wood and vinyl floors probably aren't too bad if not done to excess. A marble floor would probably be the ultimate in slick surfaces. Bubbles are best done outside the church when the newlyweds are leaving.

Can You Hear Me?

It was time for the best man to propose the toast. When he was offered the microphone, he declined. He thought his loud voice would carry across the room. He proceeded with the toast but no one in the rear of this fairly large hall could hear him.

. . . . .

My Advice: Insist that the speakers use a microphone. Mention this ahead of time. If they refuse, then they're probably not the right person for the job.

CATCHING SOME HEAT

The bride had reserved a function hall that had been recently acquired by new owners. She didn't think she had anything to worry about because the new owners had been in the wedding and catering business for quite some time. The wedding day arrived. It was a perfect sunny early spring day. The hall had many windows with southern exposure. The sun beamed through the windows and heated up the room. It became quite uncomfortable, especially for the people sitting at tables near the windows. When someone asked if the air conditioning could be put on, the manager responded, "The air conditioning is out of order!"

. . . . .

My Advice: This is a classic example of new owners booking a banquet facility before it is can accommodate guests comfortably. The new owners inherit all the problems associated with the facility. It was an older building and an entirely new system was required. The lack of air conditioning at this particular banquet facility lasted well into the wedding season. As it turns out, this bride was not alone with her "too hot for comfort day". When booking a facility, especially a recently purchased one, make sure you ask all the basic "what if" questions. Continue to be inquisitive until you're satisfied with the all the answers. Be particularly concerned with situations that could impact your comfort.

In the Raw

The function hall and restaurant was owned and operated by a famous chef who also ran a well-established culinary arts school. The students would cook meals for banquets under the supervision of the owner's daughter. This would enable them to gain first-hand experience in the world of culinary arts. They would be graded for this while working off part of their tuition. The main course, consisting of stuffed chicken breasts, was brought out. This was served to the wedding party and all the guests. It wasn't too long before the majority of the diners discovered the chicken breasts were still raw in the middle.

. . . . .

My Advice: This was a major disaster. Once the meals were served and partially eaten, they could not be brought back to the kitchen and cooked more thoroughly. Unlike a steak dinner, chicken is not served rare. Only the cooked areas on the edge of the chicken could be eaten. The culinary arts students blew the assignment and the owner's daughter didn't provide enough supervision. It's amazing how many culinary arts schools co-op with function halls and fancy restaurants. When negotiating with such a place, be sure to ask what guarantees you have that this won't happen to you. What controls are in place? Try to observe another wedding taking place there prior to your wedding. Does everything seem in order?

CHOCOLATE FONDUE SURPRISE

The bride's dad was the head chef at a fancy restaurant where his daughter's reception was taking place. Knowing how his daughter loved chocolate, he had secretly planned to surprise her with a chocolate fountain. So, after the main course was served and cleared, the wait staff set up a special table with large, succulent strawberries and melted chocolate. The bride was thrilled with her dad's unexpected surprise. The bride and groom were the first to approach the dessert table. The groom, being a perfect gentleman, picked up a large toothpick, skewered a very large strawberry and dipped it into the liquid chocolate. He then proceeded to feed his new bride. As she leaned forward to take a bite, the strawberry fell off the toothpick and rolled down the front of her dress. This made a horrible mess. She immediately burst into tears and ran to the ladies room with the maid of honor in pursuit. The groom was completely shocked and embarrassed.

. . . . .

My Advice: Perhaps the bride should have fed herself. Perhaps the groom should have been a little more careful with the dessert plate he had held haphazardly under the strawberry. Fortunately, all the formal group photos had already been taken. What started out as a little surprise turned into an unpleasant experience. Make sure you use extreme caution when dealing with potential mess makers.

DOESN'T THAT TAKE
THE CAKE!

The newlyweds and the wedding party arrived at the banquet hall only to find out that the bride's cake hadn't arrived yet. The bride's mom had handled those arrangements. She made a frantic call to her friend, the one she had hired to make the cake. "Where's the cake?" she screamed. "What do you mean? The date you gave me is next week!" The baker had the wrong wedding date in her appointment book.

. . . . .

My Advice: This is a classic example of not paying attention to the details. All the key wedding personnel should be contacted about a week before the wedding to review the details. Several calls were made to local bakeries to find out what was available. They located a smaller cake that was just baked on speculation of a sale. In this case it was quickly adorned with a wedding cake topping and delivered to the function hall in time for the cake cutting. When all else fails, a sheet cake from a local supermarket or bakery just might save the day.

DON'T DO ME
ANY FAVORS!

A platter of wedding favors sat on a small decorative table along with the guest book. The favors were small white hearts with the names of the newlyweds boldly etched into them. A nearby sign said, "Please take one!" The sign didn't say exactly what they were, but they looked like white chocolate hearts. Several guests seemed to be confused by this until one person picked one up and bit into it. It turned out to be a bar of soap. The totally embarrassed guest quickly found a napkin in which to spit it. Nearby guests who had witnessed the event chuckled quietly.

. . . . .

My Advice: This was obviously an unpleasant surprise. Little signs, strategically posted, can elicit the desired response. In this case, the sign was not explicit enough. You must clearly state what an item is and how it is to be used.

ENGRAVING THE PEWTER PLATE

The newlyweds had decided to have a large pewter plate on the gift table near the guest book, for all the guests to engrave. The guests signed the book with ease, as to be expected. When when it came time to sign the pewter plate with an engraving pen, it turned into a major production. The engraving pen danced all over the plate. The loud buzz of the pen disturbed the tranquility of the gift table and surrounding area. People in that area had difficulty conversing over the industrial-sounding buzz. It also took a great deal of time for each person to engrave their comments. The end result was a very sloppy, hard to read souvenir.

. . . . .

My Advice: The guests had signed the guest book. Engraving the plate became a redundant, annoying activity. Judging by the poor end result, it was also a big waste of time and money. The end result did not justify the aggravating process.

Everyone's Tripping

The bride and groom wanted to dress up the hall they were renting. They wanted a more formal look. They arranged for streamers to be attached to a central chandelier emanating to the corners of the room. They also rented chair covers and long table cloths that practically touched the floor. The overall look was very elegant, and a plain hall was completely transformed. The problem began when the guests tried to get up from the table. Their feet would get tangled in the table cloths and chair covers. More than once a table cloth was nearly yanked off the table. The room was elegant but posed a hazard throughout the day.

. . . . .

My Advice: Their decorations were not people friendly. When renting decorative items such as table cloths and chair covers, it's essential to try them out ahead of time. Table and chairs are like people. They all vary a little in size. Ask to borrow these items to see if they'll work for you. When you're faced with an important decision, ask yourself: what's more important, elegance or safety?

FAR OUT TOAST

It was time for the best man to propose the toast. The DJ handed the best man his wireless mike and he began his task. The bride and groom sat at a table for two, and the best man stood off to one side about fifteen feet away. As he spoke he drifted further and further away from the bride and groom. By the time he was done, he was twenty feet away from them. This didn't create a very intimate toast because he was practically hiding in the shadows in one corner of the room. The guests could hear him but they couldn't see him.

. . . . .

My Advice: Was this an extreme case of stage fright playing itself out? Was the best man extremely shy? Was he just nervous and trying to get out of the spotlight? Who knows? However, he did succeed in drawing attention away from the bride and groom by his behavior. By isolating himself, he also created a very poor visual record for the videographer and me as we documented the event. Quite often after the toast, there's a lot of spontaneous interaction between the toaster and those being toasted. Hugs, kisses, handshakes, tears - these are all quite common reactions.

A good solution to this problem is to have the toaster stand behind and between the bride and groom. This looks great in photos and physically unifies the event. This way, actions and reactions are all in close proximity.

FLAMING DESSERT

The bride and groom had selected a restaurant that required them to purchase baked Alaska as part of their wedding package. Baked Alaska is a dessert that is set on fire before it is served. The lights were dimmed and the wait staff lined up with their large metal platters. The dessert was then covered with liquor and set on fire. The wait staff marched into the center of the hall, and walked in a large circle like they were on a cruise ship. The flames were then extinguished, and the flame-blackened dessert was served. It still retained quite a bit of its alcohol flavor and very few guests actually ate it.

. . . . .

My Advice: When a function hall requires you to purchase a particular dessert as part of your wedding package, look elsewhere. This activity undermines the importance of your wedding cake. Your wedding cake is best when served fresh. Why spend hundreds on a wedding cake if it's only going to take a back seat to flaming charcoal? This also pads your bill and wastes your precious reception time. You shouldn't be forced to buy anything you don't want.

HALF AN ASSIGNMENT

The bride and groom had hired a non-professional videographer to videotape their wedding. He was what you would call a weekend warrior because this was not his full-time job. He worked another unrelated job during the week. They hired him because he was less expensive than the competition. He promised them a totally unedited video. This means that any undesirable scenes or occurrences would not be edited out. He tried to edit it as he filmed it, which is virtually impossible. He would also hide behind large columns in the function hall and videotape as discreetly as possible. However, whenever people accidentally walked in front of his camera, he would scowl and yell at them. He would blame them for ruining his video.

. . . . .

My Advice: When someone promises you an unedited video, don't consider it unless you have the resources to edit it yourself. Trying to edit a videotape in the camera as you shoot it is like trying to write the finished copy of a book on your first time through. It's impossible. Blaming innocent people around him was unforgivable. The truth of the matter is this videographer was either too lazy, couldn't be bothered or didn't have the resources to finesse the final product. An unedited video is absolute junk. Who wants to sit through four hours of real time video when the story can be condensed with a nice flow? Most professionals I have worked with will give you at least two edited copies, plus a fifteen minute highlight video. This is the one that will be viewed most often.

HIS AND HER TATTOOS

The church ceremony ended without a glitch and the wedding party boarded the limo. The bride and groom were to meet their guests about an hour later at the function hall. They had planned to stop on the way to the reception for tattoos with each other's name and the wedding date. They arrived at the tattoo parlor with the whole wedding party. The whole tattooing process took much longer than they thought, and they arrived at the function hall much later than expected. The wedding guests were quite annoyed by their late arrival and lack of consideration.

. . . . .

My Advice: Don't waste your time with activities that could have been done another time. Respect your guests. You're the reason they're all there. They came to celebrate with you.

HUSTLE TO BUSTLE

The wedding party was being introduced into the function hall. They were being introduced one couple at a time, with the bride and groom coming in last. This is quite traditional. The newlyweds went right into their formal bridal dance as soon as they entered. The bride had a long train on her wedding gown which was not tied up. The process of securing it to the back of the bride's gown, usually buttons and loops, is called bustling. One minute into the formal dance, the bride's train had swirled around both their legs and they had to be rescued. This is a detail that can easily be overlooked.

. . . . .

My Advice: Dancing right away after you're announced is usually a good idea. This officially opens up the dance floor and starts the formalities in a most efficient manner. However, one must pay attention to the details. Perhaps whoever was running the function failed to properly communicate this to the bride. Getting wrapped up in the bridal train is not a pretty sight and the bridal dance certainly loses some of its charm.

The bride must be given advanced notice by the function manager to bustle her gown. Fixing the train is usually the maid of honor's responsibility. If the bride insists on being announced with a flowing train, then be sure to allow a little time for her to be bustled. A quick alternate solution is if the bride drapes her train over one arm for the formal dance. There's usually a small loop inside the train to facilitate this purpose. However, a gown draped over an arm never looks as good as a properly bustled train.

IN THE LINE OF FIRE

All the singles ladies were assembled on the dance floor, awaiting the bouquet toss. The bride let the bouquet fly. As all the girls jumped for it, a very large person came down on the foot of a young girl about six years old. She cried in pain and went running off to find her mother.

. . . . .

My Advice: This activity should be restricted to age appropriate women. Letting a young child compete in this fashion is an accident waiting to happen. Restrict the competitors to at least sixteen years of age and older. The DJ or band leader can make this announcement.

TOO YOUNG

In some parts of the country, it's customary for the man who caught the garter to put it on the leg of the woman who caught the bouquet. At this particular wedding, the girl who caught the bouquet was about eight years old. The man who caught the garter was about forty years old. He proceeded to put the garter on the little girl's leg but she was completely horrified.

. . . . .

My Advice: This activity looked highly inappropriate. Equally unsuitable is when a young boy catches the garter and is expected to put the garter on the leg of a mature woman. Both situations create a very embarrassing situation for the children. To avoid this, proper protocol should be followed. Restrict the age of the catchers to either sixteen or eighteen years old, whichever you feel is more appropriate.

INCOMPETENCE IN CHARGE

The wedding ceremony and banquet were scheduled at a luxurious hotel in a big city. I met the bride and groom at the hotel one week prior to finalize the wedding plans. The banquet hall was surrounded by a balcony on three sides which would provide a high vantage point. It would also allow me to monitor all the impromptu wedding activities. The agreed plan was to have a small table set up for me on the balcony where I would be served a meal. This was also approved in advance by the manager. The

147

wedding day arrived. Once the banquet began, the meals were brought out and all the guests were served but there was no place for me to sit.

When I asked the bride and groom about the table on the balcony, they said the maître d' would take care of it. The person in charge that day was different from the person who okayed everything the week before. When I approached him about it, he said, "I'll take care of it!" The band that was performing that day were regulars at the hotel. When they took a break, the band was led downstairs to the employee cafeteria.

After half an hour, I once again approached the maître d' and asked about the table as well as a meal. I was working a ten hour day. He then led me to the employees' cafeteria. As I arrived, the band was leaving. This was rather unusual because all the contracted wedding personnel should be on the same schedule. A plate of lukewarm food was brought out and everything was self-serve, including the silverware, drinks, etc. I ate in ten minutes or less and then rushed back to the hall. As I went through the swinging doors, I was shocked to see the bride and groom cutting the cake. I grabbed my camera and caught the activity without a second to spare. Another minute and a key activity would have been missed.

. . . . .

My Advice: It was obvious that our predetermined arrangements were completely ignored. The band or the maître d' didn't care if the cake cutting was photographed or not. How could I have explained this to the bride and groom? The lack of concern at this wedding nearly ruined some of the photo opportunities. The band or function manager should have been coordinating the activities with me. Was there a miscommunication between the booking manager and the function manager. I had to haul a great deal of equipment around and had no place to sit. Quite often when you hire a wedding professional who is not on the referral list of the banquet facility, they will be treated poorly. Stay on top of this situation. Take care of your hired help and your expectations will be fulfilled.

KEEP IT SIMPLE!

The doors of the reception hall opened and all the guests were entered the hall. All the seating cards were written in Old English. This made reading them very difficult. The bride and groom's attempt at fancy cards backfired. The guests couldn't decipher the cryptic cards because they were nothing short of a puzzle. This in turn created a delay in all the guests finding the table at which they were supposed to be seated.

My Advice: I'm sure you have heard this before, "Keep it simple!" Your main objective should be having everything flow smoothly. Another wedding had a similar problem when they named tables after places they visited and dispensed with table numbers. Quite simply put, "avoid confusion and spell out the details!"

KIDS SUPERVISING KIDS

A group of about ten children were all sitting together at a large round table. They were cousins and siblings. Their parents were all in the wedding party. As is quite often the case at weddings, the children were seated together. These children ranged in age from about four to twelve years old. It was assumed that the two older children would supervise the younger ones. The menu included prime rib, so a very sharp serrated steak knife was included at all the place settings. It wasn't too long after the main course was served that the young children were seen wielding the steak knives, very awkwardly trying to cut their meat. The sight of this would make you cringe in fear. The two oldest children were embroiled in conversation and were impervious to the danger in front of them. This continued until an observant adult intervened.

. . . . .

My Advice: Children sitting with other children at a reception is certainly not out of the ordinary but four year olds using very sharp steak knives is unusual. Quite often the children will have a special menu of various finger foods such as chicken nuggets, French fries, mini burgers, etc. If this is not the case, the wait staff has no way of knowing the place settings might be inappropriate. The function manager should be on top of this and should be told where the children will be seated. This was somehow overlooked and a hazardous situation arose. Having young children supervised by an eleven or twelve year old is not a good idea. When a potentially dangerous situation presented itself, they were literally "out to lunch". When parents are unavailable due to wedding party commitments, be sure to delegate some responsible adults to supervise. Hiring a babysitter for the reception is quite often the prudent thing to do when aunts and uncles aren't available. Make the children's table safe and provide the appropriate amount of supervision for the number of children.

LANTERNS FROM HEAVEN

It was a late summer night wedding. The ceremony and the reception took place on the grounds of an historical mansion. Like many elaborate estates, this was once a privately owned residence that was now rented out for formal events by the local historical society. The ceremony took place at a gazebo on the grounds and the reception would occur inside an elaborate carriage house. Outside the carriage house was a large courtyard bordered by classical bronze and stone sculptures. A tent was erected in the center. This would provide a spacious venue for music and dancing. The bride's family elected to decorate the inside of the tent with large, colorful Japanese lanterns. Inside each lantern was a battery operated light. When lit, they created an inviting, festive atmosphere. Once the formal dances were finished, the floor was opened for everyone to join in. As the taller people on the floor danced while swinging their arms above their heads, they'd bump into the lanterns. This in turn caused the lanterns to come crashing on the floor. The festive atmosphere quickly diminished as each successive lantern met its demise.

. . . . .

My Advice: It's really amazing how something so simple can create an atmosphere or ruin it. What happened was, as the bride's mother later explained, one company set up the tent and the bride's family put up the lanterns. Later, a different company set up a four inch high dance floor and moved the tent posts out a little bit. This altered the footprint of the tent as it lowered the ceiling. This unusually high dance floor moved people closer to the lanterns. With their arms fully extended, they made accidental contact with the ceiling decorations. Whenever several different groups of people are providing different services, everyone must know exactly what the next merchant is providing and how it might impact the overall physical layout of the wedding. In this case, knowing that the dance floor was four inches thick would have encouraged the decorators to use smaller lanterns or to hang the decorations higher.

LARGE FLOOR ARRANGEMENTS

The wedding party was lined up outside the main entrance of an elaborate dining room. The formal introductions were about to begin. Inside the hall, on both sides of the entrance, were two very large floral arrangements in matching vases. The introductions began and one couple at a time was introduced into the hall. The dresses the bridesmaids were wearing were quite full at the bottom. One of the bridesmaids barely brushed against the floral arrangements and the whole arrangement came crashing to the ground. This sent chards of glass everywhere before the bride and groom were even announced. It also brought the grand entrance to a screeching halt. The wait staff scurried to clean up the mess so the bride and groom could make their entrance.

. . . . .

My Advice: The floral arrangements looked fantastic before the accident. Were they a little top-heavy or placed in inappropriate containers? Were they placed too close to the aisle? All these factors definitely contributed to this mishap. You should discuss these types of potential problems with your florist. Take a good look at the practical side of things and judge accordingly.

Lights Will Cost You Extra!

A large old gothic church was purchased by a culinary arts school. The main area with the high ceilings, barrel vault and many columns was converted to a function hall. All the pews were removed, leaving a large open expanse for banquet tables. The remainder of the structure would house the culinary arts school. The banquet hall was quite tall and dark. The lack of adequate ceiling and column lights gave it an overall gloomy feeling. Whenever an engaged couple would discuss this situation with the owners they were told, "We can light this for you, but it will cost you extra!"

. . . . .

My Advice: This facility was frequently rented. Yet they failed to provide adequate lighting for the function unless the bride paid extra. Permanent, energy-efficient lighting should have been installed and factored into the cost of renting the hall. Be very leery of any facility that wants to charge you extra for something that should be included as part of the package. Otherwise, the dark ages may return.

MIRROR, MIRROR ON THE WALL

The bride and groom retained a small, inner city hall for their wedding reception. The owners of the hall totally surrounded the perimeter of the hall with large mirrors. This would make the hall appear much larger than it was. The downside of this was every time someone took a flash photograph, they would encounter horrible reflections in the mirrors. They would also capture their own reflection in the mirror.

. . . . .

My Advice: This type of situation is very problematic. It someone were to photograph the newlyweds toasting or cutting the cake, they would experience a lot of unwanted information in the background. Granted, in this era of digital photography, retouching can be done. However, it requires a great deal of work and will generate an additional expense. Avoid rooms lined with mirrors unless you're at the fun house at a local amusement park. Simple backgrounds will not compete with you or the activity that's taking place.

MISSING CAKE KNIFE

The reception was well under way and it was time to cut the cake. The DJ announced the event and the newlyweds went over to the cake table. The DJ started playing the requested background song for the cake cutting ceremony. However, the bride and groom just stood there looking at each other. The cake knife was missing and no one knew where it was.

. . . . .

My Advice: Oops! This occurrence is not all that rare. The DJ or band leader almost always coordinates this with the function manager because the wait staff has to remove the cake and cut it up before serving it to the guests. Obviously, there was a breakdown of communication somewhere along the line. As it turned out, the knife was still in someone's car in the parking lot. While the ceremony was delayed, somebody ran out to get the knife. The function manager should make sure everything is in place on the cake table before the DJ or master of ceremonies is prompted to make the announcement. Quite often it's not the cake knife that's missing but the napkins, which is almost as bad. It results in messy faces for the bride and groom and no way to clean up.

No Polkas Allowed!

The disc jockey received specific instructions from the bride that they'd be no polkas played during her wedding reception. So after the basic formalities, i.e., the toast, the cake cutting and the bridal dance were completed, the DJ announced that the dance floor was open and that he would entertain special music requests. Shortly thereafter, the mother of the groom approached the DJ and requested a polka. The disc jockey politely declined, citing the particular orders that he had received from the bride. The groom's mom immediately approached the bride's mom to voice an appeal. The bride's mom reinforced the bride's request with, "They don't play that kind of music at weddings anymore!" The groom's mom went over to her husband and whispered something in his ear. He immediately got up and they both left the reception.

. . . . .

My Advice: Now this was obviously a very controversial issue. Was the groom's mom being unreasonable? Was the bride being spiteful to her new mother-in-law? Did her mother-in-law have a reputation for being overbearing? You could take either side in this situation and have a good argument for or against. However if you step back and take a good look at the overall picture, it seems for the sake of future family relations, a compromise would be in order. By limiting the number of polkas to one or two for the entire event, a potential family feud could have been avoided. Granted, the bride's family was probably footing the lion's portion of the bill. As the saying goes, "He who pays the piper, calls the tune!" However, a ten minute window of polkas during a four or five hour event would have secured peace. The bride could have taken a bathroom break while the polkas were being played. Remember, it doesn't hurt to be nice. Extend a little courtesy to your guests and try to make everyone feel welcome!

No Show Caterer

The bride and groom planned a wedding on a very limited budget. They rented a hall and hired a caterer to provide the food service. They arrived at the reception hall after the church service, but caterer was nowhere around. After several frantic calls, they realized that the caterer wasn't going to show up. Somehow, the caterer got the dates and times mixed up and the newlyweds would have to deal with it. With about one hundred hungry guests, something had to be done. About a half dozen family members left for the closest fast food chicken restaurant. It happened to be just down the street. Thirty minutes later, they returned with about twenty buckets of chicken, mashed potatoes, gravy, cole slaw and biscuits on the side. There was also a liquor store nearby. Another group returned with plastic wine glasses, soft drinks, wine and beer. All ate and drank and everyone had a good time.

. . . . .

My Advice: Always confirm and reconfirm all the dates, times and details. The final confirmation should be done about a week before the wedding. If you wait until the day before, you might not be able to find a replacement in time if there's a problem. This is particularly true if it's a holiday weekend or a very popular date. When a problem arises, seek out solutions. This couple turned a negative into a positive. They didn't succumb to their bad luck. Keep a smile on your face and will yourself to have a good time no matter what.

PLAYTIME FOR THE WEDDING PARTY

The wedding ceremony ended at 5 PM. with the reception scheduled for 6 PM. The bride, the groom and the wedding party wanted to stop at a local bar where they normally hung out to say "hello" to a few friends that couldn't be included in the reception. When they arrived, all their friends started buying drinks for the wedding party. Being in the mood for celebrating, they gladly obliged. By the time they arrived to their formal reception party it was 8 PM and they were pretty well inebriated. The invited guests were aghast. They waited around for two hours for the guests of honor to arrive, and what they received was a group of slobbering, cantankerous drunks.

. . . . .

My Advice: Why bother with a formal wedding reception if the invited guests take a backseat while the wedding party drinks with friends at the local watering hole? This was the ultimate affront to their invited friends and relatives. Perhaps they didn't plan to stay there as long as they did. They certainly didn't consider the possible ramifications of stopping there. Celebrating with this group of friends could have taken place at another time that wouldn't have impacted the most important day of their lives. Be considerate of your wedding guests and plan accordingly!

RAISIN CAKE

The wedding reception took place in an elaborate mansion during the hottest day of summer. As with many older mansions, there wasn't any air conditioning. Built largely of marble, the classical architecture didn't lend itself to the sheet metal duct work coming through the floors and ceilings. It was an evening wedding and the ten foot doors were left wide open to keep the place cool. The cake, a beautiful multi-layered masterpiece, was covered with butter cream frosting. You could smell its aroma from several feet away. When it was time to cut the cake, the bride and groom were called over to the cake table. Much to their horror, the raisins started moving! Their cake was inundated with dozens of very large flies that had burrowed into the frosting until they were engorged. This quickly put an end to the cake cutting ceremony and the notion that this dessert would be served with coffee.

. . . . .

My Advice: How could have this happened? Only the flies enjoyed the wedding cake. As with many mansions, the live in caretakers simply rented the building. The bride and groom had to bring in their own catering company. They were concerned with serving the food and not watching the cake. The baker could have expressed a little concern but quite often a delivery person simply delivers, sets up the cake and then leaves. If there was an official function manager or wedding coordinator, they should have been aware of this potential disaster but there wasn't one. Hindsight is always perfect. Delegating a friend or relative to take care of the cake would have been a good idea.

Covering the cake with a makeshift tent of white netting would have solved the problem. Keeping the cake in the delivery boxes would have worked as well, but why have a fancy wedding cake if you can't show it off? This insect problem can also surface at tent weddings as well.

RECYCLING AT ITS WORST

The bride and groom had rented a small inner city function hall. It was recently acquired by a catering company that was branching into the restaurant business. The newlyweds had arranged for an open bar during the cocktail hour. A large oval bar was located in one corner of the room. As I sat discreetly at one end of the bar, waiting for the next activity to begin, I noticed the bartender on duty that day (one of the new owners) was recycling drinks. Whenever someone would leave a half-full soft drink behind, the bartender would discreetly put it under the counter. A few minutes later, he'd pour it into another glass of ice, top it off with the appropriate beverage and give it to another unsuspecting guest. This continued throughout the cocktail hour. He didn't miss ringing up every drink on the cash register. His unscrupulous behavior served to pad the bill substantially while generating maximum profit.

. . . . .

My Advice: This was an extreme example of retaining a company that didn't have an established business record. These same people were also noted for watering down their liquor. Open bars are usually charged per drink or a flat fee per hour.

A flat fee should be preferred, providing they have enough bartenders to meet the demand. Consider the bartender to guest ratio. When negotiation for this service, ask for a past client referral or two. When talking to these past clients, ask them, "Were you totally satisfied with this service, or could anything have been better?"

RUNAWAY TOASTS

The reception was underway. The best man stood up with the microphone and gave an eloquent toast, honoring the newlyweds. The father of the bride then asked for the microphone and gave an impromptu toast. This encouraged the maid of honor to do the same (after all, she was the bride's best friend). Then the mother of the bride and a few other people also asked to give toasts. The toasts continued for more than thirty minutes. They became cumbersome and repetitious.

. . . . .

My Advice: Run on toasts can be quite tedious. Guests can only stand up and absorb what is being said for so long. Weddings can be dragged out and meals served at random hours. Be kind to your guests. Question all the key parties well ahead of the wedding day to find out who intends to give a toast. Once the tally is in, save a little time for a few toasts later in the reception, perhaps before or after the cake cutting.

SLIP SLIDING AWAY

The ceremony was over. The bride and groom were thrilled. They were married! They hurried out to the limousine and the driver poured them a champagne toast. He left the bottle with them so they could help themselves. Help themselves they did! They polished off the first bottle and drank a second. All this happened on the way to the function hall. A half hour later they were announced into the reception hall and proceeded onto the dance floor for their first dance. Within fifteen seconds, the bride staggered and fell on the floor. How embarrassing! She was intoxicated and obviously had too much to drink on an empty stomach. This was quite unflattering. In her haste to celebrate, she exceeded her drinking capacity. She was helped to the head table. The toast was cut short and she switched to soft drinks. The bride eventually made a recovery but only after consuming a large meal.

. . . . .

My Advice: Alcohol never makes the event. Be honest with yourself. Do you really need to drink? If so, stay within your limit. Save excessive drinking for private occasions when you're not the center of attention.

STICKY LITTLE FINGERS

The wedding cake was beautiful and on display for all to see and admire. However, the bride and groom had several young nieces and nephews who obviously weren't being supervised very well.

They all went up to the wedding cake and stuck their little fingers in the bottom layers of the cake. These were the only layers they could reach. This left numerous little furrows in the cake and one very upset bride.

. . . . .

My Advice: Some people may find this as being cute. The bride obviously did not. When young children are present at a wedding, the children need to be closely supervised or the cake must be placed out of reach. Putting cake in front of a child is too great a temptation. They will sample it!

TABLE ALIGNMENT

The wedding party was being announced at the far end of the function hall. They were to walk down a makeshift aisle created when two rows of tables were set up in parallel. At the end of the aisle was a table for two, designated for the bride and groom. Just beyond their table was the dance floor. The plan was for the bride and groom to immediately walk out to the dance floor as soon as they were announced. The introductions began and when the bride and groom were walking by their table for two, someone brushed against a chair, knocking it ever so slightly into the table. This in turn knocked over their tall wine glasses which were already filled with wine. This totally turned the head table into a soggy disaster. While the guests of honor danced their first dance, the wait staff hustled to rearrange the head table with fresh linen and dinnerware.

. . . . .

My Advice: The table was set up a little bit out of alignment, so the makeshift aisle actually narrowed at the end. The wine glasses at the head table were quite tall and prone to tipping. Perhaps their wine glasses were filled a little too soon. The room layout should have been discussed in depth with the function manager prior to the big day. It's important that the room layout is people friendly.

TABLE PHOTOS

At many weddings, the bride and groom request photographs of all the guests sitting at their tables. The only time they're all at their tables is when the meal is being served. The photographer is busy during the wedding party entrance, the toast and the blessing. This means all the guests would have to be disturbed while trying to enjoy their meal. The photographer is then perceived as a big nuisance. At this particular wedding, after the main course was served, many people were at the bar, dancing, smoking outside or in the restroom. This makes this task all the more challenging.

. . . . .

My Advice: This practice of photographing people while sitting at their tables is rather old fashioned. Many less obtrusive options are available. A large group photo can be taken inside a church if there's a balcony. The front steps of the church is another option. Any hillside, large staircase, or high vantage point would also serve the purpose. The key to the success of this endeavor is pre-planning. The guests should be notified that a large group photo will be taken at a particular time and place. Any stragglers that missed the group photos could be photographed with the newlyweds later in the day. This makes a lot more sense.

THE ARID TOAST

The reception was underway and the disk jockey gave the microphone to the best man. He then asked him to propose a toast to the bride and groom. This is a very traditional activity and the best man was well prepared. He rattled off his toast to the newlyweds and then finished with "Let's now raise our glasses!" Everyone raised their glasses except the bride and groom. In fact they looked quite perplexed. Their wine glasses were still empty and no one had noticed.

. . . . .

My Advice: This oversight happens more often than you'd realize. Sometimes the DJ runs all the activities, but whoever is communicating with the guests must also constantly coordinate the activities with the function hall manager. If the wine or champagne is poured too early, it will become warm or flat. Therefore, the bride and groom are usually served last. The maître d', head waiter or banquet manager must insure that everything is prepared and ready to go. Sometimes the newlyweds are toasting with a different beverage than the rest of the guests. They might not drink alcohol at all or they might have a favorite drink they splurged on for their wedding day. In this case, the bride and groom weren't served at all. The wait staff and DJ must be on top of these little details. It also helps when the newlyweds speak up as soon as they realize that something is amiss.

THE ARMORED CAKE

The bride and groom were both professional people. They had done quite a bit of traveling together prior to their wedding day. In their travels, they had collected quite a few unusual seashells from exotic places. They thought it would be a fun idea to have a tropical theme for their wedding reception. So they gave their shell collection to a baker and asked him to incorporate them into their cake. Their wedding day arrived and the cake looked magnificent. Real seashells adorned the cake's frosting from top to bottom.

It was time to cut the cake. The newlyweds carefully maneuvered around the shells and cut it and then it was time for the staff to serve it. That's when reality hit. The wait staff could not serve the cake in its present state covered with shells as it could be very hazardous to the consumer. Real shells posed a definite choking hazard or at least a threat to cut the inside of one's mouth. This created a liability issue. The only thing they could do was to remove the shells one by one. The shells of course were partially embedded in the frosting. When some were removed, they had a tendency to fragment into little pieces. When they were finished, what was left was not a pretty sight at all. In fact, it wasn't fit to serve.

. . . . .

166

My Advice: What were they thinking? What was the baker thinking when he accommodated their request? Logic totally evaded these people. You can't serve a cake if it's covered with sharp objects. They neglected to consider the possible consequences of a cake covered with real shells. This rendered their cake, which cost several hundred dollars, inedible. A logical solution would have been to decorate the cake with a confectionery solution, such as shells made of white chocolate.

THE BLACK AND BLUE MESS

The bride and groom had a romantic sunset engagement portrait taken at a nearby beach. This was done well before the wedding day. Their intention was to have an enlargement of this made for their wedding day. The center of the photograph would be in color and the perimeter would be a much lighter black and white image. The newlyweds would be using this in lieu of a guest book during the reception. This is normally referred to as a signature board. All the guests would be invited to sign the perimeter of the photo.

On the wedding day, the photo was placed on an easel right near the gift table. A nearby sign clearly stated, "Please sign the photograph using the pens provided!" This seemed very harmless and uneventful. However, the bride and groom had purchased the wrong kind of pens. When the guests tried signing the photo, the water based ink would not write very well. It also took quite a while to dry. Other people trying to sign the signature board would accidentally smudge the previous writings. Some guests even tried using their own blue ball point pens. The end result was a multicolored disaster.

. . . . .

My Advice: What started out as a nice idea, letting the guests create a nice wedding day memento, turned out to be a mess. Not every pen is suitable to write on a slick surface. What they needed was a fast drying, solvent based fine tip permanent ink pen. This type of marker will easily write on a slick surface. What most people don't realize is that it's easily removed from a non-absorbent surface, such as a glossy photograph, with solvent alcohol and cotton swabs. This means any undesirable comments or accidents can be judiciously cleaned up before it's framed under glass. It's also a good idea to test any writing instrument ahead on time, on a surface similar to the one on which it will be used.

THE COUNTRY CLUB WEDDING

The ceremony and reception was taking place in one location, a plush country club surrounded by rolling green hills. When the ceremony was over, the bride and groom wanted to go outside for a photo session on the grounds. It was a fantastic day and the golf course, as to be expected, was full of golfers. This created a hazardous environment, so the wedding party was restricted to inside the building or immediately around the country club.

. . . . .

My Advice: Many country clubs cater to weddings to supplement their income during the slow season. Logic dictates the wedding party can't walk in front of golfers at a golf course. For this reason, the grounds are rarely available during nice weather. Some places do make exceptions, but the areas and time frames are usually extremely limited. Most places have their own unique policies, which should be discussed when booking any location.

THE DIRECTOR

The wedding party arrived at their chosen reception location. It was a function room at a big city hotel. The function manager introduced herself and proceeded to show the wedding party and me to the designated photo area. She explained how much time they had for the photo session and when they had to be lined up for the formal introductions into the reception hall. This was all within her job description and the information she disseminated was well appreciated.

However, as the sequence of the evening's events unfolded the function manager became a little obtrusive with her specific requests, which sounded like this, "I want you to get this shot of the flower girl lying on the chair," or, "I want you to take photo of the bride's dad at the bar." The function manager had clearly crossed the line, aspiring to be the director of photography. She even attempted to tell me when I could or could not go to the bathroom. This continued throughout the evening right up until the going away sequence when the bride and groom left the function and waved goodbye. The crowd didn't follow them, so she _coerced the crowd to follow them out to the waiting limo, which created a contrived ending._

. . . . .

My Advice: It's amazing how often wedding related personnel and relatives feel it's their prerogative to meddle in another's area of professional expertise. This behavior encumbered the natural flow of candid wedding photography. Whenever this type of behavior is prevalent, the bride and groom should intercede on the part of the professional whose toes are getting stepped on.

THE DJ'S CHOICE

The wedding reception was well underway. With a half an hour before the end of the event, the disc jockey played a particular song. The function manager approached him in a real tizzy and said, "What are you doing playing that song now? That's supposed to be their going away song!" It seems that the function manager approached the bride and groom during the reception and asked them what song they wanted for their final dance. She neglected to discuss this with the DJ.

. . . . .

My Advice: Here's a classic example of professionals superseding their boundaries. It's the disc jockey's responsibility to resolve this with the bride and groom, not the function manager's. These types of details are usually resolved well before the wedding day. That is, unless the engaged couple can't make up their minds in advance. Do yourself a favor. Resolve the music details well before the event!

THE FLOOR SHOW

It was time for the bride to throw her bouquet as is customary at most wedding receptions. All the single girls, including some of the bridesmaids, were gathered on the dance floor. The bridesmaids wore strapless dresses and were positioned in front of the other ladies. The disk jockey gave the bride a count of three on which she threw the bouquet toward the girls. It was a high toss, so all the girls had to jump to try and catch the bouquet. Much to the chagrin of one of the more well-endowed bridesmaids, her breasts continued in an upward motion as she was coming back down. Her breasts popped out of her gown. She quickly pulled her dress up while a few guests laughed at her expense.

· · · · ·

My Advice: Everything is relative at a wedding. If the bride and bridesmaids were all Las Vegas showgirls, this wouldn't be such a big deal. However, they weren't and the bridesmaid was highly embarrassed. Strapless gowns are not the best outfits to be jumping up and down in. Always evaluate the situation and determine the best thing to do. You can always forego the bouquet toss, give it to a good friend or to someone you think deserves it.

THE GLOWING BRIDE

It was time for the bride and groom to cut the cake. The cake was surrounded on both sides by large candelabras on tall stands. Each candelabra held at least five lit candles. Both the bride and groom cut the cake without incident. However, when the groom fed the bride, she backed up in fear of him possibly shoving cake into her face and bumped into the candles. Her veil caught on fire, which was quickly pulled off her head and thrown on the floor. A few glasses of water extinguished the flames.

. . . . .

My Advice: Granted, cutting the cake by candlelight is a very romantic notion. But is it really worth the risk? This scene could have ended much more tragically but fortunately, it didn't. Candles contained in glass chimneys are a much safer bet. Safer still are the candelabras that contain small light bulbs.

THE LAVISH TENT WEDDING

A very large white tent of circus proportions was set up very lavishly. The tables, chairs, dance floor, band stand, bar, and lights all looked wonderful. The event began with hors d'oeuvres being served by the wait staff. At the same time two bars served drinks in plastic cups. This went on for about an hour, with the wedding party lying low elsewhere before they were to be announced. There weren't enough trash barrels in plain sight so the paper plates,

*napkins, toothpicks, plastic cups and uneaten hors d'oeuvres accu-
mulated on the tables. The event was being catered and the wait
staff was busy serving but no one was really collecting the trash.
By the time the wedding party was announced, the place looked
like a disaster.*

. . . . .

My Advice: The company that rented the tent and all the
accessories certainly could have rented a few barrels. Perhaps
the caterers could have provided more trash containers. The
trash was their responsibility because their food was generating
it. Six or eight nicely decorated trash containers placed just
outside the tent would have eliminated this mess. Be sure you
discuss trash disposal if you're hiring caterers.

The Castle Cake

*The bride and groom were smitten with a particular castle at a
famous amusement park. In fact so much so, that they wanted
their wedding cake to look exactly like that particular structure.
They found a baker who agreed to their request and promised
to create a close likeness. The wedding day arrived, and the cake
was delivered to the function hall. When the wait staff set it up,
they noticed it was shaking and wobbling whenever someone
walked by. They decided that the only safe thing to do was to
leave the top section off the castle until it was actually time to
cut the cake.*

. . . . .

My Advice: Some ideas can be highly impractical and here's a classic example of that. The bride and groom wanted that special cake and paid a lot of money for it. The design was structurally unsound. The baker should have advised them against this. Concrete and steel are sturdy building materials but cake is not. Unfortunately, the newlyweds only saw their cake completely assembled for a minute or less. Don't let your love of a building flaw your logic. Try to project what will happen in the real world.

THE OBSTACLE AT THE HEAD TABLE

The wedding party consisted of twenty people including the bride and groom. The head tables were long and were parallel to each other at the front of the room. The only assigned seats at the head table were for the bride and groom, maid of honor and the best man. They sat at the center of the table farthest from the wedding guests. The rest of the wedding party could sit where they wanted at either of the head tables. One of the groomsmen was very large and tall. As fate would have it, he sat directly at the table in front of the bride and groom. This effectively obstructed everyone's view of the couple. Whenever the bride and groom were involved in any activity, like the toast or a kiss, the guests could hardly see them because they were hidden behind a giant. This also made photo and video opportunities very challenging.

. . . . .

174

My Advice: Allowing the majority of the wedding party to sit where they wanted was certainly a bad idea. The rule of thumb should be, big people in the back or off to the side and small people in the front. This is the most practical way to organize the head table. Don't hide the guests of honor. Seat them where everyone can see them. Assign seats for the wedding party and make sure you consider guest interaction.

THE OFF COLOR TOAST

The groom's brother was the best man. He was given the wireless microphone and asked to propose the toast. He was not a public speaker and was totally unprepared. He tried to make a spontaneous toast but he was not a gifted speaker. He started babbling and stumbling during the toast. He was telling one off color story after another about the groom. This went on for a few grueling minutes with the guests squirming in discomfort. Finally, someone yelled, "Take the mike away from him and let's toast!" Someone took the mike, the toast ended and the guests raised their glasses in relief.

. . . . .

My Advice: Quite often toasts can be humorous, sincere or emotional. This toast fell into the pathetic category. Some people can't make a public toast if their lives depended on it. The groom, knowing his brother's capabilities, should have insisted he prepare a toast on paper printed in very large, bold type. If he couldn't handle this by himself, for whatever reason, then someone should be delegated to help him with this task.

THE ONE ARMED GROOM

It was late into the reception and the bride had just thrown the bouquet. A large group of single men were assembled on the dance floor, anxiously waiting for the groom to toss the garter. The DJ counted to three and the groom, standing with his back to the group of men, threw the garter. All the men jumped in unison and one lucky guy caught the souvenir. The groom immediately clutched his right shoulder and grimaced like he was in extreme discomfort.

Everyone laughed hysterically because they thought he was trying to be funny. A few minutes later, he was still clutching his shoulder, in obvious pain. Someone finally asked him, "Are you OK? What's wrong?" He answered," I've dislocated my shoulder. It happens every once in a while." An ambulance was called, and the groom was taken to the hospital. The bride remained at the reception to stay with the guests. The groom returned about an hour later with his arm in a sling. All the guests cheered. It was just in time for the last dance of the evening. So he danced with his new bride with his arm in a sling.

. . . . .

My Advice: The groom knew he was prone to dislocating his shoulder so he should have skipped the garter throw. He could have faced the group and shot it slingshot style using the stretched elastic or he could have also handed it to the person of his choice. Where was the common sense that day? His mishap worried the bride and many of his guests. The groom also lost valuable time to mingle with his guests. Consider the possible consequences of your actions and act wisely.

THE OTHER BRIDE CAN'T SEE YOU

Quite often very large hotels or restaurants can accommodate several weddings in different rooms concurrently. The bride and groom chose this particular restaurant not only for its fine food but for its picturesque staircase and elaborate chandelier. This is usually the location the bride selects to have her formal wedding photos taken. It was five minutes into one of these photo sessions on the staircase that the function manager approached the bride and said, "There's another bride arriving in a limo that just pulled up in front of the building, so you'll have to go hide with your wedding party in another room. We can't let the other bride see you!"

. . . . .

My Advice: This is outrageous. The main reason why the bride chose this location was to use the scenic staircase and chandelier. Hiding in a secluded location would totally preclude using the facility as she hoped. She wasn't late but was right on time. The function manager was totally insensitive to the bride's needs. Granted they wanted each bride to think that hers was the only function, but let's be realistic. Is one bride more important that the other? I think not. When booking a function hall that caters to many events simultaneously, ask if there's a policy on using a particular location and what the alternatives are. Twenty minutes is a bare minimum of time for group photos, contingent on the wedding party size and the cooperation level. Discuss this at length when you book the facility.

THE OVERCROWDED HALL

The bride and groom selected a banquet hall and booked it for their wedding day. Then they started to formulate the guest list, which grew until they challenged the hall's capacity. When the wedding day arrived, the hall was overcrowded. Round tables were placed too close together and the makeshift aisles were barely passable. When one person rose from their chair, they banged into the chair behind them.

· · · · ·

My Advice: This could have been a safety issue or violated state fire codes. Extremely crowded wedding receptions create major problems. Simple tasks like going to the restroom or getting up to dance become problematic. In this case, the situation got out of hand. Be realistic. Formulate your guest list first prior to reserving the reception hall. Retain a location that will comfortably accommodate your family and guests.

THE POTLUCK RAN OUT OF LUCK

The bride and groom were young and had to get married. They didn't have a lot of money so they rented a hall at the local club and asked all the friends and relatives to bring food. This is called a potluck dinner. The buffet table was set up and the food looked and smelled great. They used fuel cans under the disposable aluminum trays to keep the food warm. There was just one little problem. They didn't have trays of water under the food to create a double boiler. This would have prevented the food from burning. The food directly over the heat source was scorched. If the guests served themselves early, the food was fine. After a while, the taste of the burnt food permeated the hall and the dinner was ruined.

. . . . .

My Advice: They meant well when they started out. If they had rented double trays or chafing dishes they would have avoided the problem. People without catering experience think that they can light a candle under a heavy disposable aluminum tray. Fortunately, all was not lost that day. The guests were able to eat sandwiches and some food cooked in a crock pot.

THE REAL BEST MAN

The wedding party had just been announced into the function hall. They stood at the head table while the best man proposed the toast. When he finished, the wedding party sat down and the meal was served. Everyone was famished as the church ceremony took place several hours earlier. When the roast chicken was served, the best man quickly cut a large piece and gobbled it down. He obviously didn't chew it well enough because it became stuck in his throat. He immediately stood up and used sign language which indicated he was choking and couldn't breathe. The groom instantly stood up behind the best man and applied the Heimlich maneuver. He clasped his hands together and pushed quickly and forcefully against the best man's stomach.

This technique worked and the chicken piece went flying out of his mouth. Everyone cheered for the groom who was the hero. He had saved his best friend.

. . . . .

My Advice: Fortunately for the best man, the Heimlich maneuver was getting a lot of publicity at that time in local newspapers and magazines. Many people were getting familiar with this technique but never really saw it in action. It was a learning experience for all who witnessed the event. Who knows what would have happened if this technique was never perfected. Almost every wedding has a guest who has had medical training. Know who these people are and feel free to call on them in case of an emergency.

THE RUNAWAY BALLOONS

All the guests were seated in the function room of a large restaurant. The wedding party was lined up in the hallway just outside the main entrance, waiting to be announced. The head table where the wedding party would be seated was about thirty feet long. A beautiful, festive balloon arch was secured from one end of the table to the other with nylon filament fishing line. About three feet from each end stood a large candelabra with five candles. The function manager ordered the wait staff to light the candles. The introductions no sooner began when one of the candles melted the nylon line. Just as the bride and groom entered the room, the balloons started flying freely above the head table. Instead of a well decorated head table, the balloon *arch was only attached at one end. This was like looking at half a rainbow with the majority of the balloons hovering against the ceiling. The beautiful effect was ruined.*

. . . . .

My Advice: Balloons can certainly dress up an ordinary space. They can certainly add an upbeat, festive quality. A nylon line is the standard way to secure balloons in the decoration industry. Whoever provided the candelabras didn't pay close enough attention to where they were being placed. The function manager overlooked the proximity of the candles to the balloon arch. If they had been moved another three or four feet from the end of the table, this would have never happened.

THE SLURRED TOAST

The groom and his groomsmen were a tightly knit group. They had all played on the same hockey team in college and were accustomed to celebrating together. The groom had given them fancy silver pocket flasks at the rehearsal dinner which was their gift for being in the wedding party. They arrived on the wedding day, with their flasks filled with alcohol cleverly concealed inside their tuxedo jackets. They all took sips here and there but most of them exercised restraint. The best man, however, did not. He hit the liquor harder than the rest. When it came time for him to propose the toast, he slurred and mumbled his words. He sounded like a comedian imitating a drunk. The only problem was that he was drunk and wasn't acting.

. . . . .

My Advice: The toast was barely intelligible. No one understood what he was saying or appreciated his drunken behavior. Maybe the groom should have thought twice about giving flasks to the groomsmen. This only encouraged the best man to act out. He obviously had a propensity for drinking to excess. Knowing a person's demeanor should really impact your decision making. The best man turned out to be the worst man and barely performed the duties expected of him.

THE SPREAD OUT HALL

The wedding reception was taking place in an historic mansion. They were between two hundred fifty and three hundred guests. In order to accommodate the crowd, people were situated in at least four adjoining rooms. The wedding party, close family and friends sat in the main room with acquaintances sitting in adjacent rooms. The sound system linked all the rooms, but only the people sitting in the main room where the activities were happening could actually see what was going on. The people sitting in the adjacent rooms expressed their disappointment in not having direct sight of the bride and groom.

. . . . .

My Advice: This happens quite often in old historic buildings or small restaurants. Don't make some of your guests feel like second class citizens. Usually there is one room that is a little larger than the others or is centrally located. Take a minute to invite them into the room for the activities, even if they are standing around the perimeter with their wine glasses in hand. The room will become an arena. Have them feel like participants and not left out of the celebration.

THE TRAITOR

It was time to cut the cake. The bride and groom had agreed not to push the cake into each other's face. The bride was first to feed the groom. She abided by their agreement and fed the groom in a very polite manner. Then it was the grooms turn to feed the bride. He started out very politely, abiding by their agreement. All of his friends started cheering him on, "Shove it in her face!" they cried. The groom succumbed to this peer pressure and pushed a large piece of cake into the bride's face. The bride, still holding onto a large piece of cake, was quick to retaliate.

· · · · ·

My Advice: This is not an unusual occurrence at a wedding. The bride obviously didn't trust the groom, so she held onto a piece of cake, just in case. It's not always the groom who's the instigator in these situations. The groom normally feeds the bride first, so quite often the tables are turned. If you want to completely avoid this situation, start by cutting a large piece of cake and put it in a plate. Then proceed to feed each other using dinner forks. This keeps everything on a nice, civil level. Another alternative would be to just cut the cake and forego feeding each other.

THE WEDDING THIEF AND THE FALLING CAKE

All the wedding guests were invited into the reception hall to await the arrival of the bride and groom. A large empty punch bowl was placed on the gift table to accommodate the guests that were giving monetary gifts in envelopes. The wedding cake, which incorporated plastic classical columns, stood on a table in the next room. Everything seemed to be in order until someone dressed in a tuxedo approached the gift table, grabbed the punch bowl filled with gift cards and quickly left the building. This however, did not go unnoticed. The police were called and a description of the suspect and his car were given. Meanwhile, the cake, which was to be wheeled into the main function room, toppled over. An emergency call was made to the baker to see what could be done. The bride and groom hadn't even arrived yet and their celebration was riddled with disaster.

When the guests of honor did arrive, no one mentioned the problems because no one wanted to spoil their day. Luckily, the local police apprehended the wedding bandit a few miles down the road and recovered all the gift envelopes. The baker showed up with some extra frosting, and in no time at all, had the wedding cake looking like the masterpiece it once was. The bride and groom found out about these mishaps after the fact. They were quite pleased that everything turned out well.

. . . . .

My Advice: They say that lightning doesn't strike twice in the same place but in this case, it did. Nowadays more attention is given to the security of the gift envelopes. Larger devices such as bird cages and locking mail boxes on heavy wooden stands placed in secure areas are more frequently used. Once the guests have all arrived, the gift envelopes are secured elsewhere in the office safe. It's certainly something that requires your attention. The cake, on the other hand, was an accident waiting to happen. Whenever plastic columns are incorporated as an integral part of the cake design, the chances of the cake tipping over are greatly increased. The most stable cakes are the ones that mirror the structure of a pyramid. That is, the bottom layer is the largest, with each successive layer being a little smaller and stacked over the larger base.

The Wrong Song

The reception was well underway and the bride had just finished dancing with her dad. It was time for the groom to dance with his mom. The song started out innocently enough and they started to dance. As the song continued, the lyrics were obviously intended for two lovers and not for an adult child and his mother. Before the song was over, a certain awkwardness permeated the entire reception hall. The dance couldn't end fast enough as the guests experienced the same uneasiness.

. . . . .

My Advice: When a new song comes out, make sure you listen to it in its entirety before you select it for your wedding day. The DJ obviously wasn't too well informed, as he misinformed the groom. He could have substituted another song or terminated the existing dance sooner with, "Let's have a big hand for the groom and his mom!" You must screen your wedding songs carefully and determine their suitability so this won't happen to you.

Too Hot for Dancing

It was a hot summer day and the wedding reception was taking place in a large, well decorated tent. The length of the tent ran from north to south, with the dance floor and the disc jockey situated on the west side. During the middle of the day, the tent provided quite a bit of shade. However, as the afternoon progressed, the sun moved west and started to heat up the tent. The dance floor and the DJ were particularly impacted by the solar gain. The humidity was high and the sun made it all the more stifling. The brave people who were dancing were quickly drenched with sweat. This discouraged many people from participating in the dancing. Some people succumbed to the intense heat and sought cold drinks and respite in the shade.

. . . . .

My Advice: Tent weddings on large estates are rather commonplace and can be a lot of fun. In this case, not enough thought was given to the position of the tent. Perhaps a better location or a canopy running down the west side of the tent would have provided some relief. Large floor fans, strategically placed, could have provided some comfort. The wedding organizer should have provided barrels of iced cold drinks. If you have your wedding during warm weather, be sure to carefully consider where your tent will be and what will could happen as the day progresses.

THE TOO LARGE CENTERPIECE

The reception hall was beautifully decorated. The chairs were covered in cloth. The chandelier was adorned with large streams of fabric that ran to all corners of the room. Every large, round table had a very large centerpiece situated in the middle. Each table could accommodate ten people. The centerpieces were about three feet tall and about two feet at the widest point. It became a real visual obstruction when the guests were trying to follow any formal activities such as the toast, cake cutting, etc. It also made conversation with friends and relatives very challenging because of the obstacle in the middle of the tables.

. . . . .

My Advice: I have witnessed this type of occurrence time and time again. When meeting with your florist, try to figure how their excessive handiwork might impact your wedding. The florist would love to sell you the Brooklyn Bridge, but you must decide when the floral arrangements would be too large.

TOO MANY CAKES

The tables in the reception hall were all decorated with the same centerpiece. This was not unusual. What was unusual was that the centerpieces consisted of a two layer, nine inch cake. In addition to this, the bride had a traditional large wedding cake. When it was time to cut the cake, only the wedding cake was cut and served as dessert. The reception progressed and no mention was made as far as what to do with the cake on each table. The cakes were not given out in any ritualistic fun ceremony, as many of the centerpieces quite often are.

Five minutes before the end of the celebration, the bride announced that the party would continue at her parent's house, and that all the guests were invited. The reception ended and the bride's family was faced with the dubious task of removing all the cakes, putting them in boxes, and then loading them into their cars. The plan was to bring the cakes back to the house to be served to the guests. The cakes were unloaded and served to the guests, but nobody was interested. After all, how much cake can you eat in one day?

. . . . .

My Advice: Having too many cakes at the wedding turned out to be a burdensome idea. A few missed opportunities could have remedied the situation. First, guests at each table could have been asked to cut the cake at each table in order to serve themselves. Another solution would be to award the cakes to one person at each table. They also could have eliminated the traditional wedding cake and used the individual cakes instead.

WHAT GOES UP

The bride was positioned with her back to all the single women. On the count of three, she threw the bouquet over her shoulder without looking. It was a very high toss and all the girls jumped, but the bouquet never came back down. It was stuck in the chandelier, out of reach.

. . . . .

My Advice: It's really amazing how many times a scenario like that plays out at a wedding. If the ceiling is too low or the chandelier is too low, either forego the bouquet toss altogether or try an underhanded toss. You can also give it to the person of your choice. Not every restaurant or function hall lends itself to this type of activity. Equally disastrous is when someone catches a little bit of the chandelier and nearly pulls it down. You have to use a little common sense.

HALF A DOLLAR DANCE, OR WHERE ARE ALL THE MEN?

The bride and groom had planned a reception activity called "The Dollar Dance". This is when the band or disc jockey announces to the guests "that anyone wishing to dance with either the bride or groom may do so, but it will cost you a dollar. When the dance is over, the bride and groom keep the proceeds."

189

Now let's face it, people of all socio/economic groups get married. This activity would generate a little extra spending money for the newlyweds on their honeymoon. It also serves to get complacent wedding guests off their seats and interacting with the bride and groom.

The activity began with the bride and groom dancing together while two lines formed. One line consisted of all the women, dollars in hand, waiting to dance with the groom and the other line with the men waiting to dance with the bride. Two people, the maid of honor and the best man, stood near the beginning of the lines collecting the dollars.

The line of women was quite long and the line of men was unusually short. This didn't reflect the actual number of men attending the wedding reception. The majority of males were obviously missing. What had happened? Many restaurants and function halls have a separate room with a bar and large screen televisions. It just so happened that a local professional team was involved in a major sporting event that was being aired concurrently with the reception. This attracted the majority of the male attendees to go to the bar room for a drink and to watch the game. This is a rather common occurrence.

· · · · ·

My Advice: When planning your wedding date, why not begin by doing a search of major sporting events that might take place during the time of year you're interested in? Check the schedules of baseball or football playoffs, world soccer cup or auto races and determine if any of these events might interfere with your wedding plans. Note what time of the day the event will take place. Whether you intend to have a dollar dance or not, these events will draw people away from your celebration. If your wedding is during the day and the sporting event at night or vice versa, you'll be all right. It might be even better if there are no televisions at your reception hall. Programs can easily be recorded at home.

CHAPTER 7

GOING AWAY

A TIGHT FIT

The wedding reception was coming to an end. It was time for the bride and groom to change into their going away outfits so they could be announced for their final dance. The bride had a form fitted dress so she squeezed into it and then asked the groom to zip it up. When the bride took a deep breath as a sigh of relief, the dress ripped right next to the zipper. The bride immediately panicked until the female function manager suggested a solution. She brought out a sewing kit and sewed her right into the dress. The bride went out in the dimmed lights for her final dance and then said her goodbyes.

. . . . .

My Advice: Whether the groom was over zealous with his zipping or the bride gained some weight, we will never know. The bride should have tried on her going away outfit at least a week before the wedding. If it didn't fit, she could have left in her formal attire or could have found another dress. Pay attention to all the little details.

CIRCLE OF TEARS

The bride and groom wanted to be courteous and say goodbye to all their guests. They agreed with the DJ to have a circle of friends and family surround the dance floor during their final dance. When they returned to the reception, they were immediately reintroduced into the hall to loud applause. They started their final dance to a slow, sad song with a circle of friends *surrounding them. About halfway through the song, they stopped dancing and started going around the circle to say goodbye. It didn't take long for someone who was hugging the bride or the groom to start crying on their shoulders. Soon, the newlyweds became just as emotional as their guests. The whole mood turned into a tear jerker. Everyone had red, teary eyes, runny noses and some of the women had runny makeup. This slowed down the whole going away process. The couple had a plane to catch and time was running short. They finally made it to their waiting limousine, highly disheveled and stressed out and the limo sped off to the airport.*

. . . . .

My Advice: I'm not sure everyone who reads this would perceive this as a problem. But when you consider the bride and groom had already been through a very long day, you begin to see my point. Factoring in that time was very limited in this case and they still had a plane to catch. Suddenly, a quicker exit seems to be the better solution.

The entire day was a positive, upbeat event. Why, then, do so many weddings have to end on such a sad (blubbering) note? For some people, these drama filled moments provide a certain amount of closure. If that describes you, then be sure to make your celebration a little shorter and allow more time for a friendship circle. However, I can provide some alternatives.

First, the friendship circle can easily evolve into a "tunnel of love." This is done by the DJ or band leader, who asks, "Will all the guests in the circle now form two lines facing each other. Now join your hands above your heads with the person in front of you. The closest relatives of the bride and groom are asked to take a position at the end of the line." This human tunnel should run from the dance floor towards a designated exit point. On the DJ/band leader's cue, the bride and groom will scurry through the tunnel. They should stop briefly at the end to hug and kiss their closest relatives and then run out the door, waving and shouting "goodbye" to everyone in the room.

Another alternative would be to start the final dance as a slow song and then ask everyone to join in. As soon as they do, change the song to a fast, upbeat one. Instead of a sad, depressing goodbye, the music would create a better mood for leaving and saying goodbye. Both solutions are shorter and sweeter without all the drama and then you won't look so disheveled. Ask yourself, do you want a sad, dramatic finale or a fun, happy ending?

CLASHING OUTFITS

The bride and groom had just returned from changing into their going away outfits. They were announced into the hall to a resounding cheer. The groom wore a loud bright blue Hawaiian print shirt with white pineapples and coconuts all over it. The bride had a bright hot pink, satiny dress. The shiny material made her look larger than she really was. Any flash photos that were taken of her resulted in large, shiny reflections.

. . . . .

My Advice: Taste is a matter of personal preference. These outfits were problematic because they distorted the bride's back side and the colors of the two attires clashed. Couples go through a lot of trouble to look great on their wedding days. However, it's been my experience that not enough thought is given to the going away outfits. Lay the outfits on a bed side by side. The one that visually jumps out at you is probably the one you shouldn't use. If in doubt, ask other people for their opinions.

DADDY DON'T GO!

The bride and groom just returned into the hall for their going away dance. The groom had a six year old son from a previous relationship who attended the wedding. One could tell they were really close as attested by their constant interactions throughout the day. One minute into their final dance, the little boy ran out on the dance floor crying and tugging on dad's shirttails. "Daddy don't go!" he cried out several times in a most gut wrenching plea. The guests who had assembled in a circle around the bride and groom all became emotionally involved. He clung to his dad like he would never see him again. There wasn't a dry eye in the room as everyone's heart went out to the little boy. Finally, dad picked him up and started dancing with him and his new wife. This placated him and tears of sadness turned to smiles.

· · · · ·

My Advice: The ideal scenario would have been to whisk him away before the last dance. Fortunately, the groom had a sister who was quite close to her nephew, so she picked him up at the end of the dance. Situations like this can be avoided with a little forethought. Maybe he could have been brought to another room with other children before the last dance.

DON'T WET YOUR PANTS

The end of the wedding reception was quickly approaching and it was time for the bride and groom to change into their going away outfits. Much to the groom's dismay, he had his shirt and jacket on the hanger, but his going away pants were missing. The best man had brought in his going away outfit from the car earlier in the evening. He had run in from the parking lot because it was dark and it was also raining. The groom quickly explained his dilemma to the best man and a few friends. They quickly went on a pants hunt in the parking lot. It didn't take long to find the groom's pants soaking wet, lying in a puddle of water. The groom had to wear his tuxedo pants as part of his going away outfit.

. . . . .

My Advice: If you're planning on changing at the end of your dinner celebration, you should really bring your going away outfits into banquet facility much earlier in the event. After you have determined the entire outfits are complete including all accessories such as shoes, belts, hats, cosmetics, flowers, etc. Make sure the function manager secures them in a safe place. Then it will be one less thing to worry about.

THE DRUNK GROOM AND THE MISSING BELT

The groom and his friends were drinking shots of liquor at the bar throughout the wedding reception. When it was time to

*change into their going away outfits, the groom was so inebri-
ated he couldn't even find his belt or tie his shoes. The band
was patiently waiting for his return but they couldn't play the
last song to end the event. This would be when the newlyweds
would say goodbye to their guests. Rather than prolong the day, I
loaned the groom my belt and tied his shoes. He was now ready
to stumble through his last dance and then find a quiet place to
pass out.*

. . . . .

My Advice: Most people don't plan on getting drunk at their
weddings. When friends start buying each other drinks, it can
sometimes have an adverse effect. Many restaurants and function halls don't allow shots to be served at the bar for this reason. The prudent thing to do is to have the bar close an hour
before the event ends and serve coffee, soft drinks and pastries
as an alternative. This gives those who have imbibed too much
some recovery time before getting in their cars. As mentioned
in "Don't Wet Your Pants", the going away outfits should be
brought into the function hall or restaurant and secured in a
safe place well ahead of time. This would happen after the outfits have been checked for completeness.

THE SHAKEDOWN

*The wedding reception was running a little late as the bride and
groom said their farewells. They both went to change into their
going away outfits while a limo was waiting to take them to the
airport. The groom finished first because the bride was getting out*

of her gown. As to be expected, it is a much more time consuming process. The groom, while waiting for the bride was approached by the limo driver who said, "Look, by the time I drop you off at the airport, I'll be on my overtime rate. So if you want me to stick around, it will cost you an additional ninety dollars right now. I only accept cash."

This came as quite a surprise to the groom as the bride had made the limo arrangements and he wasn't aware of the exact details. The bride was not available because she was still changing. Reluctantly, the groom succumbed to the limo driver's not so subtle extortion. He wasn't even sure if the driver was authorized to make the collection, but if he didn't pay, the limo was leaving without them.

. . . . .

My Advice: It sounds like the limo driver was shaking down the groom for cash and would later call it a tip, not mentioning it to the owner of the company. The bride, unfortunately was unavailable at the time so she couldn't verify the legitimacy of the driver's demand. She alone knew about the limo arrangements. That's why it's so important to have a written service contract known to both the bride and groom prior to the event. The agreement should clearly state the size of the limo, what time the services will begin and what time they will end.

The availability of the limo for overtime should also be stated and what the rate will be. The contract should include acceptable forms of payment (cash, check, credit card), when the payment is due and who is authorized to accept the payment.

Chapter 7: Going Away

THE LAST DANCE

The bride and groom returned from changing into their going away outfits. They were then announced back into the banquet hall for their final dance. A large circle of family and friends surrounded the couple and they proceeded to dance slowly within the circle. The bride was carrying a very large bag as part of her going away outfit. She began dancing with this large, cumbersome bag hanging over her shoulder. This looked less than graceful and was actually a distraction. When their final dance was over, they started hugging and kissing people goodbye. The bag was still getting in the way.

. . . . .

My Advice: Try hugging someone with a mini suitcase hanging on your shoulder. It just doesn't work. The bride should have given her bag to a close friend or relative to hold for her during the grand finale. Instead she bumped and banged it into everyone with whom she came into contact. Someone could have come to the bride's rescue but no one did. Don't let this be you. A little foresight goes a long way.

UNSUPERVISED CHANGING

The bride and groom usually change from their formal attire before returning to the function hall for their final dance. At this particular wedding, the groom lived nearby, so they both left the premises to change. All the hired help [the band, the videographer and I, as well as the guests anxiously waited for their return. A half hour, then forty-five minutes elapsed and still no sight of the bride and groom. After an hour they finally showed up, hair dripping wet. At this point all the hired help was on overtime. But the newlyweds had specifically requested the going away sequence, so the hired help was obligated to comply.

. . . . .

My Advice: When newlyweds have too much privacy when they're changing out of their bridal clothes, this unnecessary delay will occur. Was it a romantic liaison or just an extremely slow couple? Who knows? This also cost the bride and groom overtime charges when the event ran beyond the predetermined time limit. Why not send the maid of honor along with the bride to help expedite things? The guests were already involved in a long day of celebration and this only prolonged it. So why not take care of the business at hand and be considerate of your waiting guests?

WE HAVE A PLANE TO CATCH!

The wedding reception finished right on time. Most function halls have their own schedule to maintain with the food service and the wait staff. The bride and groom had already changed into their going away outfits. Their suitcases were in the trunk of their car. They had a plane to catch in order to go on their dream honeymoon. So they said their goodbyes and made a hasty retreat to their car. Much to their chagrin, their car was decorated to the

hilt. Shaving cream covered the windows. The passenger compart-
ment was crammed with balloons and inflatable dolls. Ribbons
were wrapped around the door handles and the rear bumper was
adorned with dozens of cans. This rendered their car inoperable.
The bride and groom panicked and hastily tried to return their
car to a usable state. Meanwhile all the decorators watched and
laughed as the bride and groom panicked. I found out later they
barely made their flight.

. . . . .

My Advice: It's not unusual to see a going away car decorated.
In this case, there was a clear conflict of interest because the
decorators went overboard. They were oblivious of the newlyweds' tight schedule. This may be attributed to crowd mentality. When one person starts an activity, others will follow
without thinking. If you have a tight schedule, hide your car until
you actually need it. Informing any potential pranksters to leave
the car alone will help as well.

THE BELATED HONEYMOON

The bride and groom were both seasoned world travelers. When
planning their honeymoon, they decided they wanted to go to
Turks and Caicos Islands in the Caribbean. Arrangements were
made with a local travel agent. The trip they booked involved a
private charter plane which would take all the passengers to the
same destination. The travel agent provided them with a list of
what they would need to depart and return to the United States.
At that time, this consisted of a birth certificate and a picture ID

card. *The wedding day arrived, they were married and everything went smoothly. They drove to a local airport in a major city to catch their chartered flight. When it came time to board the plane, however, it was a different story. The airline required a current passport to embark on the plane. The bride was prepared; she brought her passport just in case and she was allowed to board the plane. The groom, following the instructions the travel agent gave him, didn't have his passport. He was not allowed to board the plane. This created a very dramatic situation on the plane. The groom appealed to the airline saying, "I can call my brother and he can bring it to me. It will only take about forty-five minutes." The pilot explained the situation to the other passengers.*

Sympathetic to the newlyweds' plight and specifically the weeping bride, they unanimously agreed to stand by until the groom's brother arrived with his passport. The groom called his brother and the plan went into action. His brother went to his home, grabbed his passport and raced to the airport. When the pilot announced that the groom's brother had arrived, everyone on board the plane burst into a thunderous cheer. They were all rooting for the newlyweds. This air of jubilation quickly changed when the groom presented his passport and it was his older expired passport instead of the current one. His brother, in his haste, had grabbed the wrong passport. The groom quickly exclaimed to his bride, "You go on without me, I'll catch the first plane out there tomorrow!" The blubbering bride stayed on the plane. The engines started and the plane departed. She was leaving on her honeymoon by herself. Strange but true. Many people on board the flight were emotionally attached to the situation at this time. Many were crying right along with the bride. It was a tearful flight. The groom left the next day on the first flight that he could book. Of course, he had to pay double the fare on such short notice. When he arrived at the hotel where they were staying, he found his wife sitting on the front stairs. With her was a tray with two piña coladas and two bottles of the groom's favorite beer. She was still crying but this time they were tears of joy and not tears of disappointment.

. . . . .

My Advice: The groom was obviously misled by the travel agent. There's a good lesson to be learned here. Make sure you have all your travels documents, tickets, reservations packed and secured well ahead of time. Double check all your travel requirements. This can probably be done over the internet. Of course, nowadays, a current passport is required to leave and return to the country. However, if you forgot it somewhere or you lose it, there will be major problems. Pay attention to the details and check them, such as departure times, travel documents, directions, connections, reservations, etc.

CHAPTER 8

THROUGHOUT THE DAY

A WHITE WEDDING DAY

The bride had planned a February wedding. She was engaged on Valentine's Day the previous year and it happened to fall on a Saturday the following year. The wedding was scheduled in a region where snow is possible but not an everyday occurrence. About half way through the church ceremony, it started to snow quite hard. By the time the ceremony was over, there was about four inches of snow covering the ground. The banquet facility was about twenty-five miles away and driving conditions were quite hazardous. The wedding party and all their guests did their best to get there. On the way, several vehicles were spotted that had slid off the road. This only heightened everyone's fear.

On arrival at the banquet hall, the bridal party was announced right away. No time was wasted and the entire pace of the wedding was accelerated. The blessing, the toast, the cake cutting and the bridal dance were all done hastily. Outside, it continued to snow heavily, creating a growing feeling of uneasiness because everyone still had to get home safely. As soon as the meal was finished, the guests at the banquet bid their farewell to the bride and groom. They departed in astonishing numbers. Instead of a relaxing enjoyable event, it turned into a panic stricken event that lasted about an hour and a half.

. . . . .

My Advice: Anytime you schedule a winter wedding in a location that gets snow, you're taking a gamble. In this case, the blizzard started while they were in church. Instead of a relaxed wedding banquet, a feeling of panic prevailed. These days, weather forecasts are more accurate and sophisticated. It's also easier to contact people with emails and cell phones.

Why not propose an alternate plan just in case your first plan doesn't work out? Discuss this with all key wedding personnel, the function hall, the officiator, the photographers, and even your travel agent. Ask them, "If I have to cancel the wedding due to extreme weather will I get a full credit for another date? By which date do I have to cancel?" If you're really nervous about this, you can always take out wedding insurance or plan for a warmer season.

THE CHAMPAGNE'S IN CHARGE

All the bridesmaids arrived on time at the bride's house. They were getting ready together, which is not unusual. However, the flower girl was late. Actually, her mother was late bringing her to the bride's house. The bridesmaids were drinking champagne mixed with orange juice. The bride, however, wanted her champagne undiluted. The flower girl's tardiness was making the bride very nervous, so she started drinking more and more champagne. When the flower girl finally arrived, it was time to leave for church and the bride was tipsy. The ceremony went smoothly and everyone proceeded to the reception. By the time the newlyweds arrived in the limo, the wine had really taken its toll. Instead of following the plan of having a formal photo session outside with the wedding party and families, all the bride wanted to do was stay inside and sit in the air conditioned room. The groom's requests were ignored. She continually complained about being too warm and feeling sick.

. . . . .

My Advice: The bride's irresponsible behavior in drinking too much on an empty stomach early in the day, sabotaged the reception. It wasn't until hours later that she had recovered enough to go outside for a quick photo session. The bride may have been nervous about the flower girls late arrival, but getting drunk was not the answer. If you know that any of the key people in your wedding party are traditionally late, ask them to arrive an hour earlier. An alternative would be to have them get ready at the same place that the bride's getting ready. Too much alcohol too early in the day will usually lead to big problems later on.

DIRECTIONS ARE DIRECTIVES

The bride gave printed directions to all the hired help who had to get to the bride's house early on the wedding day. The big problem was the directions were faulty. This resulted in numerous delays and phone calls to redirect the key people to the correct location. In addition, the bride's house was out in the country with very poor signage.

. . . . .

My Advice: The misleading directions resulted in many of the guests and wedding personnel getting lost. Some people don't know their left from their right. It's sad, but true. If the bride is bad at giving directions, then she should delegate the task to someone who can. In this era of global positioning systems and online maps, one must still ensure the accuracy of these directions. When a GPS can't get a satellite reading or is using obsolete maps, you're out of luck. One must also consider any local events, parades, festivals, construction, detours, closed bridges and traffic jams that may impact the accuracy of your directions. By including landmarks, driving distances, and phone numbers you can insure smooth traveling. It also helps to put signs, balloons or something else eye catching on the mail box, telephone pole or in front of the house. Simplify the directions and guide people accurately!

CHILDREN AT WEDDINGS

When young children attend weddings, they will become hungry, thirsty or tired. They may be part of the wedding party or involved in a lot of traveling. This can lead to cranky, disagreeable youngsters.

. . . . .

My Advice: To avoid this problem, why not bring their favorite foods in containers? Avoid messy foods like chocolates, raisins or grape juice. Juice boxes, milk and flavored water are also helpful. Hiring a babysitter with whom the child is familiar is another solution. The babysitter can whisk the children away to a quieter place and attend to their needs. This is especially important when the children are in the wedding party as well as their parents.

My Shoes are Killing Me!

The groom was considerably taller than the bride, so the bride bought a brand new pair of shoes with four inch heels for her wedding day. In this case, the bride was not used to wearing heels because she usually wore casual shoes for work. After about an hour into her wedding day, she was absolutely miserable. She must have said "These shoes are killing me!" a hundred times. By the time she completed her bridal dance with her husband, she took off her shoes for the rest of the day.

. . . . .

My Advice: Many brides try to look taller or shorter on their wedding day. This usually depends on the relative heights of the bride and groom. However, it's a good idea to break in your shoes before your wedding day. You shouldn't do this by going shopping or doing yard work. Wear them inside the house for at least an hour each day for several days. When your wedding day arrives, you'll be glad you did.

Obtrusive Hairstyles

The bride returned from the hairdresser with curly wisps of hair hanging over her temples on both sides of her head. This meant there wouldn't be a clear view of the bride's face. Throughout the day, the slightest breeze blowing from either direction would guarantee at least one strand of hair would be in front of her face.

Even when there wasn't any breeze, a mere tilt of the head, one way or the other would create the same problem. When this happens in bright sunlight, there's also the shadow of the curl with which to contend. This is not very flattering. It also becomes a major retouching nightmare on all the photographs.

. . . . .

My Advice: Quite often the bride will go to her hairstylist for a test run of her chosen hairdo and veil. She might ask a friend to take a few snapshots. In this era of digital cameras, it should be easy to determine if a particular hair style will be problematic. When in doubt, ask a professional photographer.

PHOTOGRAPHER VS. VIDEOGRAPHER

I was hired to take candid as well as formal posed photos throughout the day. When I arrived at the bride's home, the videographer wasn't working, he was just standing around waiting for me. I politely asked the videographer to perform his job so that when he was done, I could create my own images. The videographer declined and said, "I'll just shoot over your shoulder!"

. . . . .

My Advice: There's definitely a conflict of interest here. The still photographer controls the copyright of any of his posed shots as soon as he sets them up, even before he even records it. The videographer is hired to capture sounds and actions, as the medium suggests. It's not their job to shadow the still photographer all day creating a copycat video of the photographer's work. Each has a job to do without interfering in each other's work. Mutual courtesy goes a long way.

The still photographer should never knowingly walk in front of the videographer's camera when he's filming. The videographer, in turn, should never ruin an overview of a candid scene by becoming a visual obstruction. A good videographer is not a copycat. They think for themselves and capture all the surrounding interactions that occur when families and wedding parties assemble for group photos. This way, both the stills and the video will complement each other without duplication.

Why would the bride and groom want a video of virtually the same images? Why would anyone want the video to include still photos when they're capable of so much more? Copying is merely a crutch for people who can't think for themselves.

Note: The following story is similar in that any friend or relative can become a nuisance, slowing down the entire process.

THE ANNOYING AMATEUR

The bride and groom had hired me to document their wedding day. When I arrived at the bride's house, her neighbor, an aspiring photographer, immediately came over to the bride's home with her camera and shadowed everything I was doing. Not only was she violating my copyright, she was constantly getting in the way. She went as far as to try to direct the activity. Instead of a series of flowing candid images, the session became an overcrowded conflict. Usually, there's one vantage point that's better than others.

Competing for space can be quite awkward. During the church ceremony, she was constantly in the way. It was clear she was trying to create her own portfolio by copying my work.

. . . . .

My Advice: A truly candid activity can be documented by anyone; posed photos cannot. Sometimes, the bride or groom will give a friend, relative or neighbor permission to photograph their wedding. What they have inadvertently done is dump the amateur on the professional. A photographer who also does portraits for a living can clearly flatter almost anyone they photograph. This is done by selective camera angles, correct posing and proper use of light and shadow. When an amateur is thrown into the mix, this can greatly impact the professional's ability to do the job efficiently. Amateur cameras blink frequently to eliminate red eye, usually ruining any available light shot the professional wanted to take.

Most families know which friend or relative might be apt to make a nuisance out of themselves with their camera. If you hire a professional photographer or videographer, make sure they're allowed to do their job effectively with minimal interference from outside sources. If you want to get your money's worth when you hire a professional, be prepared to intercede when someone is hampering their efforts.

THE COLORFUL COUPLE

The bride and groom went sailing two days before their wedding. They didn't use enough sunblock and they both received sunburned faces. On their wedding day, the bride partially corrected her face with makeup. Her nose was still too red. What could the groom do, wear makeup? In all the wedding day photos, the newlyweds had burned, red complexions.

. . . . .

My Advice: Many couples attempt to acquire a tan before their wedding day. At all costs, avoid getting a sunburn. Even in this era of digital retouching, correcting a sunburn can be quite time consuming. This could even add an additional retouching charge on the finished photos. Use common sense and wear plenty of sunblock if you have to be in the sun just before your wedding day. Tanning salons and instant spray on tans might be an alternative.

THE SPLIT WEDDING

The wedding ceremony was scheduled for 1 PM in an old church on a very hot summer day. The celebratory banquet would only begin at 6 PM, with dinner and dancing until midnight. The ceremony started on time but the church was practically empty except for the wedding party and their immediate families. This situation didn't change much as a few more stragglers came in late. So, what happened?

. . . . .

My Advice: When the reception starts five hours after the ceremony, this is considered a split wedding. The time void between the two functions usually guarantees poor attendance at the actual wedding ceremony. If one factors in an old church with no air conditioning, the picture becomes clear. Also consider what time people had to start getting ready to attend a 1 PM ceremony. You can understand why this becomes a very long, draining day, especially in the heat. This is a realistic assumption, especially with the reception ending at midnight. Try to avoid this if possible, but if you can't, clever planning is essential.

The wedding party guests and their families can usually keep busy with group photo sessions and refreshments, but what about wedding guests and people from out of town? They cannot go back to their homes or hotel rooms to hang around in their wedding attire. This certainly would not be convenient unless everything occurred at locations in close proximity.

Don't allow your guests to languish during this time. They need to be entertained. Quite often the solution to this problem is to create a layover, usually at the bride's or groom's home. When this isn't convenient, then a rental hall is in order, complete with refreshments and a place to relax in a comfortable environment.

THE HUNG OVER GROOM

The groom showed up on his wedding day complaining of a pounding headache and an upset stomach. He was hung over from his bachelor party. The entire day was pure drudgery for him. He couldn't even eat his banquet meal. He certainly didn't feel like dancing. Many times he expressed his desire for the day to be over. Instead of enjoying his wedding day, he was tortured by it.

. . . . .

My Advice: It's very unusual for the groom's friends to throw a bachelor party for him on the night before his wedding. With some of his longtime friends coming from out of town, this was the only time they could get together. This is a classic example of what not to do. Do anything you can to avoid this scenario even if it means getting together weeks or months before the wedding day.

THE INJURED GROOMS

A groom had broken his foot the week before the wedding and had a large cast on one foot. He asked me to avoid showing his cast whenever possible. Another groom incurred a spinal cord injury in a surfing accident several months earlier in Hawaii. He was dressed as a Hawaiian god with a long robe to hide his crutches. The rest of the wedding party wore grass skirts, leis and the women wore halter tops.

. . . . .

My Advice: Neither groom gave up because of their physical limitations. They both went on with their wedding plans. The first groom showed true grit to continue with his wedding plans even though his foot was in a cast. The second groom showed some real creative problem solving. They both made the best of bad situations. Their positive outlooks carried the day. Don't give up on your dreams when you're faced with a challenge.

THE VERY LARGE WEDDING PARTY

Both the bride and groom came from very large families. By the time all the siblings and cousins were invited to be in the wedding party, they totaled forty-four people. This included the bride and groom plus all the bridesmaids and groomsmen. This meant any activity, even something as simple as the processional down the church aisle, would take about three times as long. Consider how this will impact the recessional, transportation, bathroom breaks, photography, being announced into the reception, bridal dances, etc. Therefore, plan on a very long, tiring day.

. . . . .

My Advice: There's usually a lot of love in these large families. They also provide many candid photo opportunities throughout the day. Not being able to exclude family members so you don't hurt anyone's feelings will lead to huge wedding parties and a lot of down time. If at all possible, try to avoid this situation, but if you can't, allow extra time for all activities, especially traveling.

THE VEST FAUX PAS

It was one of the hottest days in August and all the groomsmen were standing outside the church with their jackets off. They wore black tuxedos with black vests. It was still early in the day but they were sweltering in the outfits that someone had selected.

. . . . .

My Advice: Quite often a bad decision can definitely impact the comfort of the wedding party. In this case the groomsmen were all overdressed for this time of the year. It's absolutely amazing how often this happens. It may have been the result of going to the tuxedo shop in the middle of winter. A black tuxedo has a nice formal look, but it's a solar collector on a hot summer day. Adding a vest to the outfit creates too many layers of clothing. After all, the groomsmen are not going to be sitting under air conditioning all day. Did the tuxedo shop misadvise them? With the variety of light weight summer suits that are available today, don't over-dress. Light weight jackets, short sleeve shirts with open collars and khaki pants might be a good alternative. Think about how practical the outfits will be after a few hours in the heat.

The Too Large Bouquet

Floral arrangements are usually ordered by the bride. In fact, the bride's bouquet is quite often larger than the bridesmaids'. This defines the bride's importance on her wedding day. What many brides don't realize is that their large bouquets may become a burden. I can't tell you how many times I've heard brides complain about how heavy her flowers were.

. . . . .

My Advice: Big is not always best. The bride's stature and hand size should be taken into account when ordering bouquets. Quite often, florists want to impress people with their work, the thinking being that a larger bouquet is more noticeable. I've seen some amateur florists make bouquets as large as funeral sprays. However, a small to medium, well designed bouquet would be more practical than an oversized one.

Too Long Train

Very long trains are still coveted by some brides. This particular bride had a train that was twelve to fifteen feet long. The bride wanted to feel like a princess. What she didn't realize was how heavy the gown would be after dragging the excess baggage behind her for several hours. Toward the end of the day, she complained incessantly about the long train being heavy and cumbersome. It wasn't much fun after all.

. . . . .

My Advice: Brides frequently don't realize what they're in for when selecting their bridal gowns. Walking around a bridal salon for ten or fifteen minutes is not a real indicator of what the actual day will be like, such as getting in and out of cars, passing through narrow doorways, climbing stairs, trying to keep the gown clean and using restrooms. These all become extremely challenging endeavors when the bride's train is too long. Some trains are detachable, but this is a trendy phenomenon that might not be available when selecting your gown.

Try to project how practical your gown might feel after wearing it for several hours. Besides the weightiness of an exceptionally long train, there are also some other drawbacks. When the bride is being photographed for a full length portrait, the size of her head, looks extremely small by the time her entire gown is included in the photo. When a full length photo is taken, there's usually a feeling of wasted space around the bride. In other words, you'd wish you could see a little more bride and a little less gown. A creative photographer might attempt to drape her train over a railing, staircase or chair to compress the size of it. This usually takes too long when working in a limited time frame. Every time the bride moves, there's more gown to rearrange.

TOP HAT

The groom had a receding hairline. He thought wearing a top hat was a great idea. He could hide his baldness and dress very formally at the same time. He had also chosen a tuxedo with long tails. The problem was the hat didn't fit him very well as it was quite large.

. . . . .

My Advice: If you want to look silly on your wedding day, wear a hat that doesn't' fit you very well. For a top hat to flatter, it must be the correct size. A hat that's too big will usually rest on the ears. This causes them to stick out in a most unflattering manner. That's exactly how this groom looked whenever he wore his top hat. On the other hand, a person with a large head with a hat that's too small might look like an elephant with a cupcake on his head. Weddings with a retro theme are great fun but there are many other hat choices (floppy, fedora, gangster, etc.) that probably would have suited him better. Why not bring friend whose opinion you trust to the formal rental shop for an honest opinion?

TWO VIDEOGRAPHERS

The groom's parents were divorced and lived in different states. It became obvious they were not on good speaking terms. When the wedding day arrived, videographers from two different companies showed up, one hired by the mother and one by the father. Each had brought an assistant, which created a huge conflict of interest. Throughout the day, they vied for the best vantage point during any of the major activities. It was reminiscent of the paparazzi trying to photograph celebrities.

. . . . .

My Advice: The groom should have acted as the intermediary in this case and finalized the deal with one company or the other. If the parents don't talk to each other, someone must oversee the important details. One company, I might add, was dressed very formal and appropriately. The videographers from the other company were dressed very casually. Be sure to discuss how the hired help will be dressed. If your wedding is a black tie event, you have an obligation to let all the professionals know.

THE WEDDING FROM HELL

The bride and groom both worked for the Red Cross in Mexico. They returned to the United States to get married in New England in the middle of August. The wedding ceremony and reception would both take place in an old historic mansion that was reminiscent of a castle. There wasn't any air conditioning and all the rooms smelled quite musty. The ceremony went off smoothly in the main hall. The wedding party wasted no time getting high in their own little corner of the castle just before it was time for group photos. Everyone was preoccupied with laughing and joking. The bridal party wasn't very cooperative. What should have been a twenty to thirty minute photo session turned into pure drudgery.

Shortly afterward, the meal was served. The wedding party sat in the main dining room with the majority of the guests. The overflow of guests who couldn't fit into the main dining room were seated outside in the courtyard. As the evening went on and the sun went down, the guests in the courtyard encountered a few unpleasant surprises. Creatures of the night such as mosquitoes, moths, flies and an occasional bat dive bombed the guests in the courtyard. They ate quickly and hastily retreated back into the castle. There was no respite from the unbearable humidity. This in turn made their clothes stick to their bodies until their skin chafed. When the event ended, the guests left the premises in record time.

. . . . .

My Advice: This certainly doesn't sound like fun, does it? This couple would have been better served with a smaller, casual type setting in a more comfortable environment. The guests and relatives were basically tormented every step of the way. As it turned out, the bride's parents wanted one type of wedding and the bride and groom another. What ensued was pure hell. This supports the notion of visiting an unknown function hall about a year before your wedding date, especially if you can peek in on someone else's wedding. This will let you know what you can expect.

FINAL QUIZ

QUESTIONS

Please note: This quiz should be used as a guide for planning your own wedding. The answers to these questions are based on my personal observations after attending over fifteen hundred weddings in a thirty-five year time span.

1. Question: Why should brides be extra cautious going through doorways and getting in and out of cars?

2. Question: When are aisle runners impractical?

3. Question: Why are rose gardens not a wise choice for photo sessions?

4. Question: Why should outdoor locations that are designated for wedding party photos be carefully inspected before the bride and bridesmaids disembark from the limousine?

5. Question: When is a fireplace not a wise choice for group photos?

6. Question: What precaution should be taken when a horse and buggy brings a bride to her actual ceremony location?

7. Question: Why should any formal photo session take place earlier in the day or right after the ceremony?

8. Question: Why should going away outfits be checked and secured early in the wedding day?

9. Question: Why is it never wise to have too many limo stops between the ceremony and reception?

10. Question: Why should driving directions be checked for accuracy right up until the wedding day?

11. Question: Why should a newly opened restaurant, banquet facility or country club be given extra scrutiny?

12. Question: If anything begins to go awry, what's the best possible solution?

13. Question: When is it impractical for the groomsmen to wear a vest or cummerbund?

14. Question: Why is it important to have only one receiving line?

15. Question: When is a toast complete?

16. Question: Why would a dress with spaghetti straps require a special floral arrangement?

17. Question: Why is it always a good idea to have an alternate location for outdoor formal wedding photographs?

18. Question: What are the disadvantages of hiring a horse and buggy on your wedding day?

19. Question: What are some of the concerns when hiring an antique car for traveling on your wedding day?

20. Question: Why are checklists so important on your wedding day?

21. Question: What hazards do the family pets pose when they're not isolated away from the wedding activities?

22. Question: Why should young children at weddings be supervised and entertained by a mature adult?

23. Question: When you wedding day is running late what is the first thing to eliminate?

24. Question: Why should restaurants or function halls affiliated with a culinary arts school be given extra scrutiny before booking your wedding?

25. Question: Why should someone be delegated to round up the people that will be involved in the formal group photographs.

26. Question: Why should the bride and groom discuss with the person that will be officiating their wedding the content of their sermon?

27. Question: What precautions should be taken when a novice officiator will be conducting your wedding ceremony?

28. Question: When selecting someone to officiate at your wedding why is it so important to see an actual wedding that they've done?

29. Question: What are some of the drawbacks of retaining a super large limousine for your wedding day?

30. Question: What wedding morning glitch can quickly bring a bride to tears?

31. Question: What is the number one reason why a bride is late on her wedding day?

32. Question: Why should the florist be asked if there's any precautions that should be taken with the flowers?

33. Question: Why should the bride be the first one styled at the hair salon?

34. Question: What are some of the drawbacks of having a metal plate and an engraving pen for the guests to use at a wedding reception?

35. Question: Why should the bride wear her bridal shoes around the house prior to her wedding day?

36. Question: Why should the bride and bridesmaids scuff the leather soles of their shoes prior to the wedding day?

37. Question: Why should friends and relatives that the bride hasn't seen in a long time be encouraged not to visit her when she's getting ready?

38. Question: Why should all wedding day arrangements be reconfirmed at least one week prior to the wedding day?

39. Question: Why should limousine drivers have extra keys in their pocket?

40. Question: Why should harsh direct sunlight be avoided during the wedding ceremony and for formal group shots?

41. Question: What announcement should the officiator make prior to the wedding ceremony?

42. Question: Why should the videographer be asked not to situate their tripod in the middle of the center aisle?

43. Question: Why is it a good idea to have a master list of phone numbers of all the key wedding locations and personnel?

44. Question: What is an abbreviated receiving line and why is it the smart thing to arrange?

45. Question: What are the drawbacks of having a formal photo session at a carousel?

46. Question: Why is it important for the photographer and videographer to have a mutual respect for each other's space?

47. Question: What is a good alternative to annoying the guests during the meal by having the photographer taking photos of each individual table?

48. Question: Why should special photo request lists be given to the photographer well before the wedding day?

49. Question: How should these photo request lists be organized?

50. Question: What extra precautions should be taken when requesting photos outside in frigid temperatures?

51. Question: Why should soft drinks and snacks be provided to the wedding party in the limo prior to taking formal group photos?

52. Question: What precautionary questions should be asked when retaining a historic location for your wedding day?

53. Question: What problem would an oversize top hat create on the groom or groomsmen?

54. Question: Why is it important for the disc jockey or the master of ceremonies to talk with all members of the wedding party before they're announced into the banquet hall?

55. Question: Why is it important for the wait staff at a function hall to know exactly where young children will be seated?

56. Question: Why is it so important to inform all the hired help that the wedding reception will be a black tie event?

57. Question: What precaution should be taken when a chocolate fountain is present at the wedding reception?

58. Question: What problems would an unedited video create?

59. Question: Why should the bride's gown be bustled before her formal bridal dance with her husband?

60. Question: Why should extremely fancy seating cards be avoided?

61. Question: What problem would the excessive use of mirrors in a small hall create?

62. Question: What precautions should be taken when you have a wedding cake in an outdoor location or an indoor place without screens on the windows or doors?

63. Question: What precautions should be taken when you have large floor arrangements?

64. Question: Why should real seashells not be used to decorate a cake?

65. Question: Why should bridesmaids with strapless gowns avoid participating in a bouquet toss?

66. Question: Why should the going away outfits be tried on at least a week before the wedding?

67. Question: Why should a young child not be present for their parents' final dance?

68. Question: Extremely large centerpieces on tables can cause what problems?

69. Question: Why should the bride and groom avoid extreme sun exposure just before their wedding day?

70. Question: Why should black tuxedos and vests be avoided during the hottest days of summer?

FINAL QUIZ

ANSWERS

1. Answer: These are the areas where a bride, will most likely pickup grease or dirt on her gown. An extremely vigilant Maid of Honor that assists the bride with her gown is the best defense against this.

2. Answer: For outdoor use on bumpy, rocky, hilly or wet grounds. On a windy day or when the bridesmaids are wearing spiked heels.

3. Answer: Thorns greatly outnumber the roses. They can wreak havoc on a bride's veil or train. The bushes make a rather skimpy background for photography.

4. Answer: Because wild and domestic animals (ducks, geese, dogs, etc.) quite often contaminate the ground with their droppings.

5. Answer: When the fire is lit and roaring or when the fireplace mantle is covered with distracting objects that will project behind the head in photos.

6. Answer: After the bride disembarks, the horse and buggy should be driven away from the actual ceremony out of earshot. Horses notoriously do gross and inappropriate things at the most inopportune time. Animals will surely act and sound like animals.

7. Answer: Because most often, the longer you wait the less co-operative the wedding party will be. They'll be in the party mode quite often imbibing alcohol.

8. Answer: Because it's too easy to lose an accessory or have it damaged. If there's a problem that's only discovered at the last minute, then it's much more difficult to come up with a solution.

9. Answer: Stops and traveling most always takes more time than anticipated. Quite often wedding guests are in high anticipation for the newlyweds to arrive. Avoid unnecessary stops for cigarettes, alcohol, makeup, etc., by purchasing the items ahead of time. This would allow you to keep on schedule.

10. Answer: Unexpected construction, detours, poor signage, parades, events, changing traffic patterns will wreak havoc on all the guests not familiar with the area.

11. Answer: Because the personnel who work there might be unfamiliar with wedding protocol and activity sequences. A relative novice might be running the show. Also find out if all the basic comfort systems will be working (air conditioning, rest rooms, backup generator etc.)

12. Answer: Be strong and project a positive attitude. Be gracious and keep smiling. If you try to turn a negative into a positive, you usually can. You'll carry the crowd and they'll reward you with applause.

13. Answer: During extremely warm weather this adds an additional layer of unnecessary clothing.

14. Answer: Time on your wedding day must be used efficiently. Redundant activities must be avoided.

15. Answer: When the person proposing the toast gives the guests an audible or visual cue to raise their glasses and imbibe.

16. Answer: Skinny straps are too flimsy to support the weight of a pinned on corsage. A wrist corsage would be more appropriate.

17. Answer: Inclement weather or unexpected events can sabotage a location. An indoor location as a backup plan will solve the problem.

18. Answer: Horse travel is slow, dangerous and unpredictable. They quite often perform bodily functions at the most inopportune time.

19. Answer: Is the vehicle comfortable? Does it have air conditioning? Can it keep up with other limousines? Does it smell fresh inside? Will a large wedding gown fit comfortably inside?

20. Answer: With so much excitement and confusion it's easy to forget an important item at the wrong place. Flowers, marriage license, rings, clothing, toast glasses and cake knife are just a few examples of things typically left behind.

21. Answer: They can jump on the brides' gown, leave fur on clothes, urinate in unexpected places and grace the lawn with droppings.

22. Answer: Older kids usually don't supervise young children effectively. Snacks and entertainment will help keep the very young in check.

23. *Answer:* The receiving line, as the bride and groom will feel obligated to visit each and every guest at their respective tables. So the greetings and welcomes will be exchanged anyway.

24. *Answer:* Quite often students inexperienced at weddings will be working off their tuition. The person supervising them must be extra vigilant, as disasters are more prevalent.

25. *Answer:* The photographer can't be working with the groups efficiently and be looking for group participants at the same time. Someone familiar with the respective family should be doing this.

26. *Answer:* Because the content must be wedding appropriate. It shouldn't include someone's personal or political agenda. Spontaneous speeches rarely work.

27. *Answer:* You must find out if they know all the basic facets of a typical wedding ceremony. If in doubt, a printed outline is imperative so that nothing will be missed.

28. *Answer:* It always helps to know the demeanor of the officiator. Some will treat it like a Las Vegas show all the while calling attention to themselves. Others will fall flat with a "let's get it done as fast as possible" attitude. You need to find someone that fulfills your expectations.

29. *Answer:* Very large limousines have difficulty negotiating narrow streets in older cities or historic districts. They'll also bottom out on steep hills, speed bumps and dirt roads.

30. Answer: There's many glitches that would do this but the most common occurrence is when the bride received a bouquet that's totally different than what she ordered.

31. Answer: Based on thirty-five years of observation, the cosmetologist doesn't allow enough time for the work that has to be done. Of course, if either the bride or the cosmetologist was late getting to the designated location that would certainly contribute to this problem.

32. Answer: Flowers can be hazardous to outfits with sharp flower stems puncturing veils, pollen rubbing off on gowns and water spilling out of baskets.

33. Answer: Because the bride usually takes the longest to prepare with her hair and veil.

34. Answer: Engraving a metal plate is quite noisy, hard to control and quite difficult to read afterwards.

35. Answer: So they'll be broken in and more comfortable on her wedding day.

36. Answer: To make them less slippery and less accident prone.

37. Answer: Their interaction will definitely delay her and she'll most likely run late.

38. Answer: To make sure everyone is still on the same schedule.

39. Answer: In the event they get locked out of the limousine, a major nightmare will be avoided.

40. Answer: Harsh light creates harsh shadows on faces and washes out subtle details on wedding dresses.

41. Answer: "Please turn off all cell phones."

42. Answer: He will become an obstacle for those wishing to walk by and a visual obstruction for guests wanting to see the ceremony.

43. Answer: When a copy of this is given to all the key people, emergency problem solving will be facilitated.

44. Answer: This is a greeting line with just the bride and groom, their parents and the honor attendants. This saves a lot of time especially when you have a very large wedding party.

45. Answer: It's difficult for older people to climb up on the carousel platform. Many mirrors create unwanted reflections. The vertical posts create obstacles and visual protrusions in the background.

46. Answer: So they can both create a superior product without interfering with each other.

47. Answer: Large group shots taken from a high vantage point will usually capture the majority of the guests. Those that didn't make it can always be photographed in smaller groups.

48. Answer: To give him/her the opportunity to analyze the requests.

49. Answer: According to the chronological sequence of the day.

50. Answer: Proper clothing is a must, even if it means renting furs, topcoats, etc.

51. Answer: If the wedding party starts drinking alcohol too early, they will be less cooperative and the photo session will take too long.

52. Answer: What restrictions do we have in regards to the use of this facility? Is there air conditioning? How many restrooms are there? Is there adequate parking?

53. Answer: The hat resting of the ears would be unflattering and make them stick out unnaturally.

54. Answer: To make sure the names are pronounced properly during the introductions and that the lineup corresponds with the listed order.

55. Answer: So they'll have the proper place settings minus wine glasses and sharp knives.

56. Answer: This information is usually included in the formal invitation. The hired help doesn't always get an invitation as they're getting paid to perform a service on the wedding day. However, if someone shows up improperly dressed they might be asked to leave or not be able to receive any food or drinks.

57. Answer: That a large plate is held under the chocolate covered fruit when the bride is being fed.

58. Answer: The video would be long and boring in real time. Any undesirable incidents would be included.

59. Answer: If she has a substantial train and doesn't hang it over her arm, she'll be sure to be all tangled in it as it sweeps around her.

60. Answer: If it's difficult to read, and guests are confused, then finding their places and tables will take much longer.

61. Answer: You would end up with many unwanted reflections and people in your video and photographs.

62. Answer: The cake should somehow be protected from flying insects. This might include some type of netting surrounding the cake.

63. Answer: They should be unbreakable and well away from where people will be dancing and walking.

64. Answer: It would be too difficult to eat the cake without getting cut or choking.

65. Answer: Their breasts could pop out when they're jumping.

66. Answer: If either the bride or groom gained or lost weight there's still be time for alterations.

67. Answer: It's usually pretty traumatic for the child when he or she realizes that mom or dad will be going away for a while. This usually sets off an emotional tearjerker among the guests.

68. Answer: It makes it very difficult for the guests to follow along with the activities. It's also harder to communicate with people on the other side.

69. Answer: Sunburned and peeling skin detracts immeasurably from the final photo product.

70. Answer: Dark clothing acts as a solar collector, making the wearer uncomfortably warm.

Final Thoughts

My sincere apologies to anyone who might be offended by these true stories. Not all people and places who service the wedding industry are derelict in their duties. In fact the majority are quite diligent.

Just remember this: when mishaps occur, don't let it ruin your day. Remember the story *They Stooped and Rose to the Occasion?* The cake slid on the floor. The bride could have cried but instead she and the groom knelt down, cut the partially damaged cake and fed each other. The guests went wild and responded with a thunderous cheer that rocked the room. I'm still impressed to this day.

> *When you don a wedding veil,*
> *May logic and common sense prevail.*
> *When things don't seem to go your way,*
> *Bring the sunshine, save the day*
> *And when your wedding day is done,*
> *May you find solace in the sun.*

There's a certain magic when two people pledge themselves to each other. It's a contagious feeling of joy that speaks to your heart, saying that there is hope for love in this world. After all, love is simply the best emotion known to man.

Love and peace to all,

—*Tom Grandmaison*

Glossary

agoraphobia–An abnormal fear of being in public places,

aisle runner–A thin, flimsy lace like carpet rolled out prior to the bride processing down the aisle.

apprentice–A beginner; a person acquiring a trade under a master.

band–The musicians hired to provide music at a wedding reception.

best man–The groomsman who acts as the primary attendant or assistant to the groom at a wedding.

bouquet toss–The custom of the bride throwing her bouquet to all the single women.

boutonniere–A flower or flowers worn in a buttonhole or pinned to a lapel.

bridezilla–A combination of two words – "bride" and "Godzilla", indicating a woman displaying a bad or hostile attitude.

brocade–A rich fabric with a raised design woven into it.

bustle/bustling–The act of securing a bride's train to fasteners on the rear of a wedding gown.

butterfly release–The practice of releasing live butterflies. This is usually done after the wedding ceremony as a sign of good luck and prosperity.

Glossary

cake cutting–The custom at weddings for the bride and groom to cut the cake together. They will frequently feed each other a piece of cake.

candid group photos–Spontaneous photographs taken of large groups of people.

cancan–A high kicking chorus line dance originating in France.

ceremony–A set of formal acts for a special occasion.

chocolate fondue–A fountain of melted chocolate used as a dip for fruit or small pieces of cake.

circle of friends–See **Friendship Circle.**

cosmetologist–A person who applies make up to other people's faces.

crowd mentality–A large group of people with the same purpose.

crying room–A room in a church designated for crying babies and young children.

cummerbund–A wide sash worn as a waistband and adapted for wear with men's formal attire.

disc jockey/DJ–A person who plays recorded music for entertainment or dancing.

dollar dance–A dance where anyone who wishes to dance with either of the newlyweds has to pay one dollar. Basically it's a fundraiser for the bride and groom.

dove release–One or more white doves released by the bride and groom as a symbol of love and peace. Is usually done outside right after the wedding ceremony.

faux pas–French for "mistake". A social blunder or error in etiquette.

flower basket–A small basket of flowers usually carried by a flower girl.

flower girl–A little girl who carries flowers and attends the bride at a wedding.

formal attire–Clothing designed for use at elaborate parties or ceremonies such as a tuxedo or evening dress.

formal photos–Structured or posed group shots of families and friends at a selected location, usually requested by the newlyweds.

friendship circle/circle of friends–The final going away dance that terminates the wedding reception. All the guests are invited to form a circle on the dance floor with the newlyweds in the center, performing their last dance.

function manager–May also be a maître d'. The person who's in charge of the wedding reception's services.

garter–A decorative elastic band worn on the bride's left leg.

garter toss–The custom of throwing the bride's garter to all the single men.

gift bowl–A large vessel placed on the gift table at a wedding reception to collect gift cards and envelopes.

groom or bridegroom–A man who is about to be married or a man who has just been married.

groomsmen–Men who attend the groom at the wedding.

hairdresser–A professional hair stylist who shampoos, cuts and styles hair.

hired help–Wedding related personnel hired by the bride and groom to provide a service.

honeymoon–The holiday or vacation spent together by a newly married couple.

Jack and Jill shower–A party for an engaged couple at which a number of gifts are presented.

JP/justice of the peace–In some states, a magistrate who has the authority to perform marriages.

limo driver–A person hired to drive the wedding party to their destinations.

limo/limousine/stretch limo–A large, luxurious car designed to transport several people. A stretch limo may hold up to twenty-four people.

liquor shots–Straight alcohol served in one ounce glasses.

maid of honor–An unmarried woman acting as the primary attendant or assistant to the bride at a wedding.

maître d'–The function manager at a reception who supervises or coordinates the service and activities.

matron of honor–A married woman acting as the primary attendant or assistant to the bride at a wedding.

medieval wedding–A themed wedding where the wedding party and guests dress in medieval clothing.

Mendelssohn–A German composer of classical music.

off the cuff remark–An impromptu or spontaneous statement.

officiator–The person hired to perform the wedding ceremony such as a priest, minister, rabbi or justice of the peace.

paper lanterns–Decorative lanterns with an inner light source.

pep talk–A brief conversation designed to induce enthusiasm and cooperation.

photographer–A person who takes photographs, usually as an occupation.

photojournalism–The process of telling stories through photographs.

pneumatic storm door closer–An air-filled cylinder which uses pressure to close doors.

processional–The wedding party moving forward on the aisle to begin the ceremony.

reception/wedding reception–An event which takes place in a restaurant or function hall but can actually take place almost anywhere, such as private property, church basements, parks, zoos, beaches or boats.

receiving/reception line–An organized line where the wedding party formally greets the guests.

reception/function hall–A facility that serves food and accommodates wedding celebrations.

recessional–The wedding party departing down the aisle from the ceremony area.

ring bearer–A little boy who carries the rings during the wedding ceremony.

signature board–A cardboard frame with photographs or memorabilia of the bride and groom which the quests write upon.

solar collector–A surface that heats up as the sun's rays beat on it.

spaghetti straps–Long, thin shoulder straps that hold up a formal dress.

still photography–Documenting an event using single images from a camera.

suspenders–A pair of straps or bands passed over the shoulders to hold up trousers.

table shots–The practice of photographing the people sitting at each and every table during the wedding reception.

tear jerker–An incident that provokes widespread tears.

theme wedding–A wedding whose decorations reflect a unified idea.

train–The part of a wedding gown that trails behind.

transportation–Any means of locomotion from a bicycle to an automobile, limousine, horse, motorcycle, trolley, train, plane, etc.

tunnel of love–An alternative way of ending a wedding reception. It consists of two lines with people joining hands on each side. The bride and groom run through the space between the lines in order to expedite their departure.

tuxedo–A man's suit designed for evening wear, originally black with a dark bow tie.

vest–A short, tight fitting, sleeveless garment worn over a dress shirt and under a suit coat.

videographer–A person who records sound and moving visual images.

wedding ceremony–The exchange of vows and rings in front of witnesses in order to become married.

wedding factories–Banquet or restaurant facilities that produce many wedding receptions at the same time.

wedding professionals/hired help–All the people employed to provide a wedding service, such as the florist, photographer, baker, etc.

weekend warrior–An individual who provides a service to the wedding industry on weekends and works a totally unrelated job during the week.

Index

train, 13, 27, 32, 34, 69, 82,
  145, 146, 221, 222
travel documents, 205
tunnel of love, 195
tuxedo, 12, 13, 18, 19, 52,
  72, 108, 111, 123, 133,
  181, 184, 198, 220, 222
tuxedo shop, 12, 13, 72,
  123, 220

U
umbrella, 35
urine, 19, 102, 109

V
veil, 25, 26, 29, 38, 57, 58,
  69, 82, 85, 125, 172, 213
very large wedding party, 49,
  56, 77, 121, 122
visual obstruction, 92, 187,
  214

W
water, 13, 20, 25, 26, 67, 85,
  86, 109, 111, 114, 118,
  121, 123, 167, 172, 179,
  198, 211
weather, 5, 9, 35, 42, 45,
  57, 78, 93, 117, 169, 187,
  208, 209
wedding bandit, 184

wedding insurance, 209
wedding license, 73, 74
weekend warrior, 143
white runner, 69, 83
windshield wipers, 42
wrist corsage, 21, 22

www.ingramcontent.com/pod-product-compliance
Lightning Source LLC
Chambersburg PA
CBHW062209270326
41930CB00009B/1696